I0123975

THE NEW ORTHODOXY
CANADA'S EMERGING CIVIL RELIGION

BRUCE J. CLEMENGER

The New Orthodoxy
Copyright ©2022 Bruce J. Clemenger

Published by Castle Quay Books
Burlington, Ontario, Canada and Jupiter, Florida, U.S.A.
416-573-3249 | info@castlequaybooks.com | www.castlequaybooks.com

Edited by Marina Hofman Willard
Cover design and book interior by Burst Impressions

All rights reserved. This book or parts thereof may not be reproduced in any form without prior written permission of the publishers.

All Scripture quotations, unless otherwise indicated, are taken from the ESV® Bible (The Holy Bible, English Standard Version®). ESV® Text Edition: 2016. Copyright © 2001 by Crossway, a publishing ministry of Good News Publishers. The ESV® text has been reproduced in cooperation with and by permission of Good News Publishers. All rights reserved. • Holy Bible, New International Version®, NIV® Copyright ©1973, 1978, 1984, 2011 by Biblica, Inc.® Used by permission. All rights reserved worldwide.

978-1-988928-80-7 Soft Cover
978-1-988928-81-4 E-book

Library and Archives Canada Cataloguing in Publication

Title: The new orthodoxy : Canada's emerging "civil religion" / Bruce J Clemenger.
Names: Clemenger, Bruce J. (Bruce James), 1956- author.
Description: Includes bibliographical references.
Identifiers: Canadiana 20220441871 | ISBN 9781988928807 (softcover)
Subjects: LCSH: Civil religion—Canada. | LCSH: Freedom of religion—Canada. | LCSH: Church and state—
    Canada.
Classification: LCC BR570 .C54 2022 | DDC 277.108/3—dc23

CASTLE QUAY BOOKS

DEDICATION

To the next generation of Christians, for whom ministry is a deep experience in a calling that comes into its own through service in Him to others—until we hear those precious words from our Father in Heaven, who abounds in mercy and grace—"well done" (Matt 25:21).

To pastors, forsaking all and going about the Father's business,[1] be assured that Christ does not leave us alone.

"Let us not grow weary of doing good" (Gal 6:9).

To all believers, we are citizens of the Kingdom of Heaven first. Our supreme earthly social and political engagement is that of ambassadors of the Kingdom.[2]

> If I speak in the tongues of men and of angels, but have not love, I am a noisy gong or a clanging cymbal. And if I have prophetic powers, and understand all mysteries and all knowledge, and if I have all faith, so as to remove mountains, but have not love, I am nothing. If I give away all I have, and if I deliver up my body to be burned, but have not love, I gain nothing.
>
> Love is patient and kind; love does not envy or boast; it is not arrogant or rude. It does not insist on its own way; it is not irritable or resentful; it does not rejoice at wrongdoing, but rejoices with the truth. Love bears all things, believes all things, hopes all things, endures all things.
>
> Love never ends. As for prophecies, they will pass away; as for tongues, they will cease; as for knowledge, it will pass away. For we know in part and we prophesy in part, but when the perfect comes, the partial will pass away. When I was a child, I spoke like a child, I thought like a child, I reasoned like a child. When I became a man, I gave up childish ways. For now we see in a mirror dimly, but then face to face. Now I know in part; then I shall know fully, even as I have been fully known.
>
> So now faith, hope, and love abide, these three; but the greatest of these is love. (1 Cor 13:1–13)

—Bruce

Have you wondered about the new sectarianism that threatens to marginalize the Christian faith? This book explains the emergence of this new orthodoxy. Bruce Clemenger challenges the arrival of a new politics that undermines Canada's commitment to religious freedom. This is needed reading for any who hope to engage in the public good with religion in heart and hand.

—Lorna Dueck
CEO of The News Forum, former Context TV host

Clemenger has long been a faithful and steady voice and mentor to pastors. Seeking to forge a thoughtfully constructive way through the sometimes turbulent, ever-changing, and unpredictable waters of the Canadian political scene, many turn to Clemenger's voice of reason, wisdom, and unique perspective. This is a definite read for any who desire to understand the shift in the relationship between faith and politics in Canada.

—Garry James
Pastor

Bruce J. Clemenger invites us into a full and careful examination of where Canadians have come from and the dramatic changes in our concepts of values, religious and constitutional freedoms, and the role of the state.

—John Reimer
Former Canadian Member of Parliament

No government in history, whether absolutist, dictatorial, totalitarian or party political, has governed without a guiding philosophy, of whatever type, whether religious or secular. As Bruce J. Clemenger clearly demonstrates, secular philosophies function in the same way as traditional religions—a religion or creed in all but name. Bruce has bravely brought to the public gaze the hypocrisy of progressive Liberalism.

—John Langlois, Order of the British Empire
Advocate

ACKNOWLEDGMENTS

To my *Faith Today* editors these decades, thank you for your skills and patience. My consistent and ever explainable late submissions would have driven most mad, but not you. You understood what I was doing elsewhere.

To Valerie Hunter—my executive assistant, your professionalism and great attitude are so affirming.

To Julia Beazley, Beth Hiemstra, and Rick Hiemstra, thank you for the many conversations over the years about political engagement that honors our faith. Thank you, Beth, for your comments on an earlier draft of Part Two.

To the EFC staff and board and many volunteers, colleagues, and members of the EFC and WEA, the Interfaith Conversation, and Military Chaplaincy—you know who you are these decades. Thank you.

Thank you, Brian and Lily Stiller. Brian, you hired me, a young lad still finding his way, and gave me the opportunity to follow in my calling through the EFC.

Thank you to my "more" extended advisers, comrades, and praying partners alongside in the journey, and to our friends in media, you know who you are. Thank you.

Thank you to the *Evangelical Review of Theology* (ERT), for permission these twenty years later to reprint my essay that now makes up Part One.

To my nurturers and friends in the days of my youth, where extremely fond memories remain—Toronto Avenue Road Church with Rev. and Mrs. A.W. Tozer; Bayview Glen Church with Arnold and Francis Reimer, Mike and Debbie Wilkins, William and Heather McAlpine, Marv and Lois Penner, and Rob and Myrna Gowing; the Bayview Glen Quartet; families from Glen Rocks and Muskoka Woods; and professors at York University and the Institute for Christian Studies.

To Larry Willard, Marina Hofman, and the Castle Quay Books team—my publisher and editors, thank you for your expertise, patience, and care.

And to my family—thank you. My calling and service opened doors that I was invited to follow into, expanding what we mean by family.

To my parents by marriage—thank you for loving me. Marriage is the first adoption, and you adopted me fully, and wow!—never a negative word but always encouraging me.

To Tracy, thank you for everything. You shared the ebb and flow alongside me, mused among the questions with playful curiosity—sometimes thorny and unfair to us both—on life, love, and callings. With joyous awe before God and under the heavens, and still with the ground beneath your feet, you kept your laughter, wit, and optimism always in your pocket.

CONTENTS

PREFACE

What does faithful Christian witness entail for individuals, churches, and organizations seeking to influence the formation of law and public policy in a liberal democracy? Liberal democracies claim to be secular in that they do not justify laws or policies based on one of the array of worldviews or belief systems to which their citizens adhere (they are nonsectarian), and they do not play favourites among these views (they are impartial and fair). Liberal states claim to follow principles and procedures that can be affirmed by a religiously diverse citizenry. The goal is to treat citizens equally and maximize their freedom to pursue their vision of the good life and of human flourishing to the extent this is possible without infringing on the same freedom for others. However, the state is not neutral and often is sectarian in its statecraft.

In this book, I present a biblically based model of public and specifically political engagement and a defense of religious freedom. From this vantage point, I examine the founding nonsectarian approach to Canadian statecraft that accommodated religious and cultural diversity. The promise of political liberalism embraced in Canada was to provide a philosophy of government that facilitates the individual's vision and pursuit of the good life. In recent decades, the promotion of individual autonomy and fraternity by governments and the courts threatens to undermine the very freedom governments claim to promote and protect. There is an increasingly secularist state which advocates sectarian principles and values that contribute to an emerging civil religion.

This book is written in two parts. Part one is an essay I wrote in 2003, the year I became President and CEO of The Evangelical Fellowship of Canada (EFC). I review the type of liberalism that dominates Canadian courts and Parliament and I examine various approaches to Christian political engagement, the role of the church and draws upon the approach taken by the EFC. I envision how Christians and churches can engage positively and decisively in a liberal pluralist state.

In part two, I draw upon my firsthand experiences working on a wide variety of issues of church and state across the tenure of six prime ministers. In the course of engaging among Christian leaders, leaders of various faith communities, with politicians, and the media, appearing before numerous Parliamentary committees and in overseeing sixty court interventions, thirty at the Supreme Court of Canada, I recognized the emergence of a new regime of liberalism which is increasingly sectarian. A cause for deep concern, it promulgates a new orthodoxy with influence beyond the political sphere and into society—akin to a civil religion. This emerging form of liberalism challenges the nonsectarian approach as it promulgates a set of principles and values drawn from a specific understanding of human nature and human flourishing. It presses dissenting views out of the public square and privatizes religious expression while undermining the original promise of liberalism to promote religious freedom.

Canadians face a choice between two liberal regimes; a sectarian regime of liberalism promoting a new orthodoxy that presses the privatization of religious expression and demands the public adherence to a prescribed set of values, a civil religion, or a liberal pluralist and nonsectarian approach conducive to freedom of conscience and religious freedom. This choice alone cannot be left to judges, politicians, businesses, or media influence; it is a principled decision to be made by all citizens in stewarding a healthy democracy.

PART 1

FAITH, THE CHURCH, AND PUBLIC POLICY: TOWARDS A MODEL OF EVANGELICAL ENGAGEMENT

Reprinted with permission by the World Evangelical Alliance from *Evangelical Review of Theology* 27 no. 2 (April 2003): 155–172, with slight modifications.

INTRODUCTION

In 1989 Francis Fukuyama announced in an article in the journal *National Interest* that we had arrived at the end of history.[3] The ideological war was over. A "remarkable consensus concerning the legitimacy of liberal democracy as a system of government had emerged ... as it conquered rival ideologies like hereditary monarchy, fascism and most recently communism."[4]

Though there were still battles to be fought in some countries, the ascendancy of a liberal vision of life and society was assured, and history, the drama of the clash between competing ideological and philosophical ways of life, was over. Twin forces within liberalism—scientific rationalism and the struggle for recognition—would lead to the collapse of tyrannies and drive us relentlessly toward establishing liberal democracies as the "end state of the historical process." The realization of the core liberal principles of liberty and equality—both political and economic—would result in a form of society that Fukuyama associates with German philosopher G.W.F. Hegel, a society which satisfies humankind's "deepest and most fundamental longings".

While many would question whether liberalism can claim victory over all other philosophies of life, others continue to grapple with the implications of this liberal vision of life for religion and non-liberal ways of life—consider books such as *Jihad vs. McWorld* and more recently *The Lexus and the Olive Tree*.[5] When we consider themes of globalization, secularization, capitalism, universal civil, political and human rights, and consider modes of influence such as the multinational corporations, the World Bank, the IMF, UN agencies, and international tribunals, we must reflect on the spirit, the worldview, the philosophy, or the vision of life that guides these.

In what follows, I examine liberalism as a philosophy or, in the language of American political philosopher John Rawls, a comprehensive doctrine. Liberalism is the predominant comprehensive doctrine in the West and is the driving force behind globalization, political reform, economic growth, and social change. I then explore the nature and purpose of the state and the political role of the church in a differentiated society, and end with a model for Christian engagement in a liberal democracy, drawing on our experiences in Canada.

LIBERALISM

I begin with some comments on liberalism. I briefly examine its core principles and how these principles have evolved. I also look at its spirit or ethos, which I describe as being religious in nature. Due to the predominance of liberalism in the West and its influence around the world, it increasingly shapes the context within which we seek to engage politically. Liberalism considers the fulfilment of individual desire to be the highest good.[6] Two characteristic principles of liberalism are freedom and equality.

A helpful introduction to the topic is found in Mark Dickerson and Thomas Flanagan's *An Introduction of Government and Politics*.[7] They identify four aspects of liberalism: personal freedom, equality of right, limited government, and consent of the governed. Freedom, they say, is usually framed in terms of individual freedom and is understood as "the absence of coercion in all areas of human life"—social, economic, political, and religious. Equality of right means we are all to be regarded as equal and to be treated equally in law and public policy. It is important to understand that these and the other aspects of liberalism's principles are not static, and how freedom and equality are understood continues to evolve. Freedom is no longer framed merely in terms of freedom from coercion (negative freedom), but is understood in terms of our capacity to pursue our chosen good. If you have no choices, can you be considered free?

Likewise, the equality of all persons before the law has shifted to equality of opportunity which carries with it a claim to positive action by others (including the state) to ensure all are equal. This is a demand not only that one's dignity as a person be respected, but also that one's choices be respected. I am not accepted as equal unless I and the choices I have made are respected and even celebrated. Politically, this shift from negative freedom to positive freedom means that the role of the state moves from a minimalist one, which leaves the individual alone unless others' rights are violated,[8] to a more participatory state; here the concern is not only the absence of coercion but the presence of means or capacity necessary for the expression of freedom.[9] The shift from legal equality of personhood to equal respect for choices (affirmation and even celebration) likewise requires a more interventionist state through the development and enforcement of human rights codes and programs and policies that ameliorate inequities.[10]

Thus the primary role of government has changed from enforcing basic rules and preventing people from harming each other through force or fraud (a "night watchman" state) to promoting freedom in the sense of capacity, and ensuring social welfare (they identify leisure, knowledge, security), and reducing differences in order to ensure that no one is prevented by others from having a chance to achieve success. The dilemma for liberalism is that the pursuit of freedom and equality are often in conflict. This conflict, both between the earlier and later definitions of freedom and equality respectively, or between the two principles themselves, is expressed through the formation of political parties which differ in their interpretation of these principles and the relative priority they assign to each.

As noted, the two other principles characteristic of liberal democracy are limited government and the consent of the governed. Dickerson and Flanagan note that the former means that there is a recognition of spheres or areas of life into which government should not intrude. One example of such a sphere is religion, which is usually understood within liberalism to be a private matter. Limited government is also expressed in a commitment to freedom of speech and freedom of the press. Consent of the governed reflects an understanding that public authority resides in the people, who delegate it to the sovereign. Taken together, the government is understood to be bound by law, which is shaped by agreement among citizens. As former Canadian Prime Minister Lester B. Pearson stated,

> Liberalism includes the negative requirement of removing anything that stands in the way of individual and collective progress. The negative requirement is important. It involves removal and reform; clearing away and opening up so that man can move forward and societies expand. The removal of restrictions that block the access to achievement: this is the very essence of Liberalism. The Liberal Party must also promote the positive purpose of ensuring that all citizens, without any discrimination, will be in a position to take advantage of the opportunities opened up, of the freedoms that have been won.[11]

The four principles of freedom, equality, limited government, and consent of the governed are not problematic for Christians. Certainly, we affirm freedom and equality, and we recognize the value of democratic processes and of limits on government power. However, the liberalism described by political theorists such as John Rawls and Jurgen Habermas is more than a set of principles. It is variously described as an ideology or philosophy, but I prefer to refer to it as, in the words of John Rawls, a comprehensive doctrine.[12]

Liberalism's prime commitment is to individual autonomy understood as individual self-determination. It seeks to remove any and all barriers that hinder autonomy. It is atomistic in that it understands the individual to be the locus of authority and meaning. Only individuals have ontic or moral status, and social institutions are but ideas in our minds, names and concepts given to associations that are nothing more than an aggregate of self-determining individuals who cooperate because they share a common interest or purpose.

All social institutions have only a derived, and therefore tentative, contractual existence. Their authority and power over the individual are carefully delimited. Forms such as the family and the state are deemed necessary but are considered man-made and artificial entities. They are considered potential threats to the autonomy of the individual. Thus the family is merely an interacting framework for developing the rights and abilities of each family member, marriage is merely a contract which is binding as long as the participants agree, a business is an artificial entity in which economic transactions take place among freely competing individuals, and a church is something akin to an ethnic association and is formed for the private benefit of its members.

Within liberalism, society is seen as an aggregate of self-determining individuals tending autonomously and automatically toward a state of natural autonomy, and the state is an instrument through which rational self-determining individuals can be assured of having their basic liberties protected. Political order exists solely to safeguard the purposes of autonomous individuals. Justice is understood to be rooted in intuitive ideas and can be identified apart from any appeal to the good. The rational person, in establishing what justice is, can distance themselves from their religious and cultural context and function as an unencumbered self who is autonomous (able to choose ends) and is an individual (identifiable apart from their religious and cultural rootedness).

Hence within a liberal understanding of life, while we function privately (or nonpublicly) as members of families, of cultures, of religions, publicly we gather as citizens, leaving these other attachments behind and affirming our ability to choose our own path—described by Nietzsche in terms of "lifestyle" and "values". At our core it is believed we are separable from these other attachments. It is to this core self that liberalism appeals. As indicated already, liberalism has a spiritual or religious thrust. Eric Voegelin describes it as having a revolutionary impulse that is expressed in four areas: the political, economic, religious, and scientific.[13]

Politically, it is defined by its opposition to certain abuses and opposes any order based on privileged position. Voegelin says the problem is that while this attack was originally led by the liberal "bourgeoisie" itself, the attack on privilege turns on the bourgeoisie, and the revolutionary movement cannot end until society has become egalitarian.

Economically, it seeks to repeal legal restrictions that set limits on free economic activity and believes there should be no principle or no motive of economic activity other than enlightened self-interest and that all barriers (including national ones) to trade and economic progress should be eradicated.

Religiously, liberalism rejects revelation and dogma as sources of truth; it discards spiritual substance and becomes secularistic and ideological.

Finally, scientifically it assumes that the autonomy of immanent human reason is the source of all knowledge. Science is free research liberated from authorities, not only from revelation and dogmatism but from classical philosophy as well. As a revolutionary movement it continues to press for reform and, according to Voegelin, it will not result in a stable condition until its goal is achieved. It continues to press towards an "eschatological final state", characterized by true freedom and equality. Voegelin says:

> One can't get away from the revolution. Whoever participates in it for a time with the intention of retiring peacefully with a pension which calls itself liberalism will discover sooner or later that the revolutionary convulsion to destroy socially harmful, obsolete institutions is not a good investment for a pensioner.[14]

This prioritization of individual autonomy as self-determination and the accompanying rights is presumed by many liberals to be enlightened, reasonable, and without bias towards most comprehensive doctrines to which citizens may adhere. It is considered uniquely public in that it is applicable to all and benefits all, and is not the product of any one comprehensive doctrine. It forms the basis for what John Rawls calls a public conception of justice that guides public life. As this view of the person and conception of justice are seen by liberals such as Rawls to be independent of any given comprehensive doctrine, they are seen as secular (nonsectarian) and political, not philosophical. They are principles to which all reasonable citizens can agree. As such, they provide a political framework able to accommodate a plurality of reasonable comprehensive doctrines.

However, this "overlapping consensus" presumes that these liberal conceptions will guide public life and that public dialogue will be guided by public reason, that is, reasoning that is nonsectarian and accessible to all citizens. Thus while comprehensive doctrines inform nonpublic life, the expectation is that all citizens are expected to function publicly as liberals.[15]

Religiously rooted arguments are perceived as being suspect and an indication of an attempt to impose one vision of life on all citizens. Law and public policy must be defended in terms of public reason. Liberalism is more than a commitment to certain principles. Following James Skillen, if we define religion as human convictions, presuppositions, and commitments that give fundamental direction to human actions and moral arguments, liberalism would qualify. Skillen writes,

"The deepest presuppositions of so-called secular philosophies function in the same way as do the deepest presuppositions of traditional religions."[16]

The Enlightenment and Communism, he says, "by this interpretation are as religiously profound and comprehensive as any outlook fostered by a historical religion ... No argument about bad law or good law can proceed without reference to normative ideas of authority and freedom, of human dignity and responsibility." By this analysis, political liberalism, like all political/legal systems around the world, has its historical origins in a particular "religious" vision of life. Even so-called secular approaches to political life, says Skillen, are themselves thoroughly religious in nature. The guiding spirit of liberalism is the pursuit of freedom (and equality) and entails a specific understanding of human nature, or normativity, and of knowledge. As a comprehensive doctrine, it shapes people's perceptions of themselves and societal institutions, conforming both to its understanding of truth.

POLITICS, THE STATE, AND RELIGION

Religion or faith is a dimension of all of life, including government and the state. As persons we are creatures of God, and our lives are lived in response to the Word of God—that by which the world was created and by which the world is sustained. (Culture is an expression of this response.) As faith is an aspect of all of life, all that we do has a faith dimension—whether we eat or sleep, in our role as parents, or in our politics. All that we do has a religious dimension. This understanding rejects the notion that part of our life is lived in the secular realm—a realm of activities that are areligious or neutral with regard to religious belief. Likewise, all that we do has a political dimension—office politics, negotiating with a spouse and children, and so on.

Politics involves power, authority, coercion, influence, and conflict resolution. It involves gathering and maintaining support for common projects; it concerns disagreement and conflict as well as the distribution of good things such as wealth, safety, prestige, recognition, influence, and power. These concerns are not limited to the state. All institutions or societal structures involve these political issues— family, schools, business, voluntary associations, and religious institutions.

The elements of politics are the exercise of power (influence, coercion, authority) and justice, and these apply to all human relations and social structures. However, it is the government and the state for which politics is the core dynamic (Rom 13). Governing is a specialized activity of individuals and institutions that make and enforce public decisions that are binding on the whole community, and it "bears the sword" (Romans 13:4). While other institutions in society exercise forms of coercive power—family/parents (punishment), churches (excommunication), schools (withhold degree), business/unions (firing, strikes)—the government retains power of life and death. Governments cannot depend solely on coercive power, however, or their legitimacy will be eroded.

Stated another way, the state is a creature, an entity instituted by God, and, like others such as the family or the institutional church (as distinguished from the body of Christ), it is created and designed by God to serve God in the fulfillment of its given task. We are told that the governing authorities are God's servant to do good. It has a unique structure, different from that of the family, the church, a school, or a business, and, like all of these structures, we can speak of it having a spiritual direction. A family can be a Muslim family or a Hindu family or a Christian family. While the structures may be similar, the faith commitment and the spiritual orientation of the families will differ. Likewise with ecclesiastical institutions, and, I argue, with the state. All states have executive, legislative, and judicial functions. Similarly, all states are directed by something variously described as an ethos, a vision of life, a worldview, a philosophy, or a faith perspective.

When I speak of the state as being religious or faith-directed, I am not advocating the fusion of the church and state. The church and state are distinct institutions, both of which have a spiritual direction. As institutions with different purposes and roles, they should remain separate and each respect the calling of the other. The direction of the state is identified through its political creed, often found in constitutional preambles or in its various charters.

This understanding of the state also suggests that the state cannot be "neutral" with respect to religion and culture. For example, the official language(s) or national holidays reflect the predominance of certain cultural or religious influences. Most modern states seek to be accommodating of cultural and religious (directional) plurality, and to the degree that they can do so, they are considered secular.

While describing a state as secular is usually understood to mean that the state remains neutral with respect to the various religious beliefs adhered to by its citizens, its faith perspective means it will not be without bias. States vary in their ability to accommodate deep religious diversity. To the extent that the state is not confused with the institutional church and does not see its role as enforcing that which is properly the responsibility of the church (doctrine for example), then it will be properly secular (nonsectarian) in that it retains its separation from any one church.

However, this is different from a secularist view that maintains that the state should be areligious and denies that the state has a religious dimension. This secularist approach results in attempts to restrict religion and the religious beliefs of citizens to private life, and is often characteristic of liberal states.

CHRISTIAN APPROACHES TO THE STATE

How then do we engage politically as Christians? There is no shared evangelical understanding of, or approach to, politics and the role of the state. In his book *Christ and Culture*, H. Richard Niebuhr presents five typologies that describe the different orientations of Christians to culture.[17] Applied to politics, the first orientation, which he labels "Christ against culture", entails a general rejection of culture—usually associated with the Anabaptist tradition. The church is set over and against the world, and we, as Christians, are to come out from among them and be separate. The church is an alternative community and the state, through its role of restraining evil, provides order and fairness. While its task is God-given, nothing about it is distinctively Christian. The gospel is about love and personal redemption, while politics is about worldly issues that are necessary but not of prime concern to Christians as Christians. The state is neutral with respect to the gospel, and sometimes in tension with the commands of Christ, but it is still a realm of possible Christian involvement.

The second orientation, "Christ and culture in paradox", characteristic of many evangelicals, identifies with the tension of being in the world but not of it. Politics and government deal with earthly pursuits that are part of the human condition. We try to keep our minds on spiritual things. In this view, the things of Caesar are different from the things of God. Yet the spiritual can influence the natural or material, and Christians can offer moral guidance to the government. However, the things of this world are not of prime concern. Being a missionary or pastor is a higher calling than that of a lawyer or politician. We engage politically out of concern for moral issues, implying that matters of the economy and budgets, for example, are not moral issues.

The third, "Christ above culture", is a characteristic Catholic synthesis where Christ adds a moral or spiritual dimension to life—grace added to nature. We are by nature social beings, and

> society is impossible on the human level without direction in accordance with law. Beyond the state is the church, which not only directs men to their supernatural end and provides sacramental assistance, but also as the custodian of the divine law it assists in the ordering of the temporal life; since reason sometimes falls short of its possible performance and requires the gracious assistance of revelation, and since it cannot reach to the inner springs and motives of action.[18]

The state is essentially a good one if it provides an orderly society that is compatible with the free practice of the Christian faith and the protection and enhancement of family and church life.

The fourth, "Christ of culture", often associated with a Lutheran/Anglican perspective, is characterized by accommodation. Culture is understood to be basically Christian. Politics and government are in need of redirection and redemption and this need guides Christians in their dealings with government. (Consider a situation where the head of state is also the head of the church.)

The fifth and last, "Christ transformer of culture", is a characteristically Reformed approach where the goal is the reconciling of all things to Christ, including the political. The Christian task is to bear witness to Christ in all areas of life, as Christ is Lord of all.

There are several problems raised by Niebuhr's analysis. First, while these typologies are helpful and do capture some of the orientations different Christian traditions have held, the problem is that they are characterizations. It is difficult to fit any one neatly into one category.

Second, most prefer to see themselves as transformers of culture and cast others into other categories. A key question is, what are the means of transformation: individual action, church action, and/or advocacy through Christian organizations? The characteristic Reformed approach, for example, can involve the formation of Christian schools, unions, and political parties. While these are ways of participating in education, business, and politics in a distinctively Christian way, setting up alternative Christian institutions can also be interpreted as a retreat from the world. Is this the case, or is it simply a matter of a different way of being "salt"?

Third, the opposition of Christ and culture is a false and misleading one. We were commanded in the Garden of Eden to be fruitful and to subdue the earth. Is our culture not our answer to that command? Culture is itself a religious expression, an ordering or basic pattern of living shaped by our basic beliefs.

I have found elements of these five orientations to be present in the way evangelicals engage politically. Depending on the issues, Canadian evangelicals sometimes get frustrated with the progress of secularization and say we should give up on politics—we have lost the war and we should retreat and focus on evangelism. Some may consider our legal system to be fair and principled and thank God for our Christian heritage, while others seem to think a Christian witness hinges on whether the Lord's prayer is recited at the opening of public meetings.

In general, while many evangelicals experience the tension of the Christ-and-culture-in-paradox orientation, when seeking to participate in public debates, they reflect elements of the Christ-against-culture, the Christ-above-culture, or the Christ-transformer-of-culture orientation.

In the next part of this paper, I focus on these three, the Anabaptist, Catholic, and Reformed approaches, using representative authors to explore each position, and then compare them.

ANABAPTIST

John Howard Yoder, in "Christian Witness to the State,"[19] begins with the presumption that the state's main purpose is to sustain the social order by restraining evil through exercising its power of the sword. While this is the state's God-given mandate, Yoder's pacifist position means that a Christian cannot threaten or take away the life and liberty of another; thus a Christian will find it difficult to participate in governance. He describes two ages that coexist but differ in terms of direction. The present age is characterized in terms of sin and the coming age is the redemptive reality where God's will is done.

The task of the church is to point forward as the social manifestation of the ultimate triumph of God's redemptive work. States are used by God to maintain order and to punish one another. The state maintains peace so that the church can fulfil its task of evangelism. The basis of the church's witness to the state is its understanding of the state function within the redemptive plan. The witness is indirect through the example of the church, an alternative society which demonstrates what love means in social relations. The direct witness of the church involves voicing concerns to the statesman. In speaking, Christians are mindful that most rulers are not committed Christians and that there is an incompatibility between nonresistance on the one hand and responsibility for normal government process on the other.

There are two ethics at play—the ethic of discipleship, relevant for believers, and the ethic of justice, which is concerned with self-preservation and maintaining a stable social order. This second ethic is all one can ask of the broader society. Christian witness is expressed in terms of specific criticisms concerning specific problems and these, if followed, would lead to another set of more demanding criticisms.

For example, Christians do not call for the establishment of the perfect society but rather for the elimination of visible abuses. Christians ask that the least violent and the most just action be taken. However, of all the alternatives presented to the statesman by the Christian, none will be good in the Christian sense—they will only be less evil. The Christian works towards a minimum level of wrong. All communication is addressed to individuals and is in the form of a call for an individual response. The prior concern is for the welfare of the statesman as a person. All communication is in a sense pastoral. What the Christian addresses is the gospel in relation to the present situation of the statesman. The task is to call the statesman to an act of obedience that may cause him to re-evaluate his position and choose to make a step of faith.

CATHOLIC

Jacques Maritain is a Catholic thinker who participated in the drafting of the United Nations Universal Declaration of Human Rights. In his book, *Integral Humanism*,[20] he describes Christian engagement in terms of three planes of activity. The first is the spiritual where we act as members of the mystical body of Christ. This plane concerns the things of God and includes liturgical and sacramental life, work of virtues, and contemplative action. It is the plane of redemption, the plane of the church itself.

On the second plane, we act as members of the terrestrial city and are engaged in affairs of terrestrial life. This is the realm of the things of Caesar, that of the intellectual, moral, aesthetic, social, and political. These two planes are distinct but not separate, as all things submit to the power of Christ. There are, however, two common goods—spiritual and temporal. On one level we act as Christians as such; on the second we act as Christians engaging in the world.

The third plane is intermediary—the spiritual considered in connection to the temporal. In this zone, truths applicable to the temporal are connected to the revealed truths that the church has as a deposit (custodian). This is the plane that joins the spiritual and the temporal. On this plane the Christian appears before men as a Christian as such. This is the plane of Catholic action in collaboration with the apostolic teachings of the church. To defend religious interests in the temporal, Catholic civil action intervenes in political things. It would, however, be contrary to the nature of things to demand in the second plane a union of Catholics or a Catholic political party. In the political realm they do not function as Catholic politicians, but as politicians who are Catholic.

In both the Anabaptist and the Catholic views, there is a presumption of dualism. Both identify two realms in which the role of the church and the individual differ depending on which realm they are engaging. Here distinctions are maintained between the sacred and the secular, between the spiritual and the temporal. Politics concerns the latter, the mundane. There is no distinctive Christian vision for politics. Politics is at best a neutral area of Christian participation, like that of business, and at worst it is a worldly affair, one in which it is difficult to maintain an effective Christian witness. Being a Christian politician means you bring an ethic to your work, just as being a Christian student or a Christian business person means you are honest and trustworthy. The political is not something that you understand differently from other politicians (or citizens for that matter).

REFORMED

Within the Reformed approach, the believer is fully participative and fully engaged in redemptive work in all areas of life. There is no one realm or one set of activities that are more spiritual or more holy. The book *God and Politics*, edited by Gary Smith, brings together essays of supporters defending four approaches to reformed politics operative in the United States: Christian America, National Confessionalism, Theonomy, and Principled Pluralism.[21]

For the purposes of this paper, I focus on the two that have most influence in Canada, the first and the last.

In the *Christian America (Canada)* perspective, the Christian heritage of the country is emphasized, and the task of Christians is to revitalize it. Christian principles and values are understood to have shaped the laws and practices of the country. A Christian consensus shaped the structure of society, and Christianity was granted special status under law. Secularization and humanism have eroded this heritage, and actions should be taken to restore the explicitly Christian convictions in the government. The model for this position is Rome under Constantine. Laws need not conform to the laws of the Old Testament (the Theonomist position), but instead, biblical principles and the Ten Commandments should inform and serve as the basis for law.

This view entails a notion of a Christian commonwealth: a society structured to provide for the general welfare, taking Christian standards for what constitutes welfare and as the guide for attaining welfare. It is the role of a civil government to establish and promote biblical standards in legislation and law enforcement. Through democracy legislation is not imposed, rather Christians seek to persuade. Other religions would be tolerated and permitted to worship freely, but public blasphemy would be illegal. In sum, Christians persuade society as a whole to adopt laws that are consistent with basic biblical principles.[22]

Principled Pluralism rejects isolationist, accommodationist, dualist, and dialectical positions in favour of one that is transformative. We live in a network of divinely ordained life relationships, and we fulfil our callings within a plurality of communal associations. Scripture presents universal norms that are applicable to all aspects and activities of life. These norms guide how we structure culture and our institutions such as the state, the family, and the church. As Christians we seek to reform the state in accordance with biblical norms. The task of the state is to promote public justice in society. Justice is defined in terms of office: the state should safeguard the freedom, rights, and responsibilities of citizens in the exercise of their offices. Every human has the right to a just and equitable share in the rich resources of God's creation: to life, liberty, and a responsible exercise of their office. The state must also avoid partiality and serves as the public defender of the poor and the powerless, and it safeguards religious freedom for all citizens.

Principled pluralists reject the view that the origin of the state lay only in the redemptive purpose of God or that it lay in the order of preservation in which the task of the state is essentially negative. Rather, the state is located in the normative order of creation. The state is limited in its scope and its responsibility.

The four Reformed approaches agree that a Christian view must not be imposed. They also agree that there is an integral relation between Christianity and politics and that God requires civil officials to conduct their affairs as his servants. Christians should promote biblical principles in political life through persuasion, and all agree on the toleration of all faiths and on the positive role of the state. However, they disagree on the biblical view of justice—is it the Mosaic code (Theonomy), rights and responsibilities to exercise office, or enforcing the Ten Commandments? These Reformed positions provide four models: Israel, Constantine, the Puritan, and the pluralist.

The Anabaptist, Catholic, and Reformed approaches differ in the understanding of the role of the state and the nature of Christian engagement in the political realm. They do, however, agree that the task of the church is to call the state to adhere to biblical principles. Their goal is to persuade government officials of the benefit of policy that is consistent with biblical norms.

CHRISTIAN POLITICAL ENGAGEMENT
Understanding the Context

When engaging politically, it is important to identify and understand the philosophy that has shaped and currently directs the political/legal foundation of your country. Canada is a very tolerant and peaceful society,[23] yet it is one of the most ethno-culturally diverse countries in the world with its multicultural character enshrined in the Canadian constitution.

While Canada, like European countries, was deeply influenced by the Christian tradition, it is becoming increasingly secularized and, particularly with the Charter of Rights and Freedoms enacted in the early 1980s, directed by a decidedly liberal ethos. The religious nature of liberalism drives individual autonomy (self-determination) and equality through what Canadian political philosopher Charles Taylor calls the "politics of recognition", or what I characterize as a third impulse of liberalism, the move from freedom through equality to fraternity. Individual autonomy, the equality of all persons, and the recognition (and affirmation) of difference guide the interpretation of the guarantees of life, liberty, and the security of the person found in the Canadian Charter.

For example, in 1988, former Justice Wilson of Canada's Supreme Court wrote in a case about abortion, "The theory underlying the Charter [Canada's Charter of Rights and Freedoms] is that the state will respect choices made by individuals and to the greatest extent possible, will avoid subordinating these choices to one conception of the good life." Thus the goal of the Charter is to maximize a person's autonomy. Note that this argument implies that this view of self-determination is not itself tied to any one conception of the good. It is presumed to be neutral with respect to competing visions of the good life. Ten years later, the majority of the Supreme Court, in a case about the inclusion of sexual orientation into a provincial human rights code, wrote,

> The concept and principle of equality is almost intuitively understood and cherished by all. It is easy to praise these concepts as providing the foundation for a just society which permits every individual to live in dignity and in harmony with all. The difficulty lies in giving real effect to equality. Difficult as the goal of equality may be, it is worth the arduous struggle to attain. It is only when equality is a reality that fraternity and harmony will be achieved. It is then that all individuals will truly live in dignity.

The Court not only wants to maximize autonomy, but it also affirms that true equality demands the acceptance of the dignity of others, not just in their personhood but also in the choices they make. This affirmation of all choices is what toleration is now understood to entail. Interpreting freedom and equality in terms of individual autonomy as self-determination results in a privileging of critical choice, the ability of the individual to choose between visions of life, an over-expressive freedom, and the ability to fully express one's religious beliefs.[24]

This emphasis is not only on the ability to choose, but also the capacity to move one's adherence from one comprehensive doctrine to another—with the attendant implications for the integrity of religious communities and the task of public education. As well, policies that are shaped or influenced by religious arguments are rejected. Thus in Canada, provincial legislation titled "The Lord's Day Act" was struck down by the courts while similar legislation titled "One Days Rest In Seven" was deemed acceptable. And when Canada's Supreme Court upheld the sanctity of human life, the Court noted that it meant this in a "secular" sense. Public arguments must be secularized to be considered, and religion is relegated to the private sphere.

The Role of the Church

Christian political engagement can be expressed individually, through the participation of the institutional church, through advocacy organizations and Christian political organizations and movements, or through political parties. For the purposes of this discussion, I focus on the engagement of the church. Here I am speaking of the church as an institution, not the church as the body of Christ.[25]

As an institution, the church has a specific calling. While this calling will have a public and specifically a political dimension, the church is not primarily a political organization when understood in terms of government and public policy. In terms of the institutional church's political task, the church has several roles—such as the prophetic, the teaching, and the reconciling roles. I will focus on its prophetic role.

The church, motivated by its understanding of scripture, calls the state to its task of public justice and encourages the state to govern in a way consistent with biblical principles. In this role, the church can remain non-partisan in that it does not lend public support to a specific political party or to specific candidates for office. Similarly, when the church supports or opposes legislation, it targets the principles of the legislation, not the government or public officials that sponsor the initiative. And when commenting on court decisions, the focus is on the decision and not the judges.

While there may be situations when the church may need to become partisan, a nonpartisan approach keeps the church's participation focused on principles. This focus on principles is an approach consistent with the Anabaptist, Catholic, and Reformed view of the role of the church in politics. The church is not attempting to mobilize votes for or against parties or candidates, but rather to persuade elected officials, judges, civil servants, and citizens in general of the merits of public policy being rooted and shaped by biblical principles.

This approach is fitting for political participation in a religiously pluralistic society. While the principles articulated by the church are biblical, many of these principles are shared by other faiths and often undergird law and public policy. A difficult question is in determining the extent to which the church in its articulation of principles can seek to recommend specific policies such as, for example, proposing penalties for crimes or appropriate levels of funding for social programs.

THE EVANGELICAL FELLOWSHIP OF CANADA'S APPROACH TO PUBLIC POLICY

Political engagement of The Evangelical Fellowship of Canada can generally be clustered under four themes: the sanctity of human life, care for the vulnerable, family integrity, and religious freedom. Under the theme of the sanctity of human life, we address issues such as abortion, reproductive and genetic technologies, and euthanasia. Under care for the vulnerable, we address poverty and homelessness, and refugee issues, as well as child pornography and prostitution. Family integrity involves definitional issues (marriage, family) as well as questions concerning the role of the state in supporting the institution of the family. Religious freedom focuses on the religious freedom of individuals and the freedom of religious organizations, in particular their ability to self-define. Many of the issues we address under these last two themes involve protecting these areas of life from encroachment from the state.

As indicated, the principled approach seeks to identify the biblical principle, show how it has been recognized in law, and explain the implications if violated. I illustrate this with an example in the area of euthanasia. The pro-euthanasia and assisted suicide movement is growing quickly in Canada. Recent polls indicate that the majority of Canadians now favor legalizing assisted suicide when the patient is terminally ill. The arguments for changing the law invoke the freedom of the individual to control their own life (self-determination).[26]

In the case of assisted suicide, some disabled or terminally ill persons have argued that since suicide is not a criminal offence, and since disabled persons do not have the ability to kill themselves the way able-bodied persons do, the law against assisted suicide prevents them from doing what able-bodied persons can do. Religious arguments advanced to oppose euthanasia are rejected as an imposition of one's beliefs on another and as unsuitable for sustaining law and public policy.

When appearing before a Parliamentary committee on these issues, we began by arguing that Canada was founded on and shaped by a vision of life which is characterized by specific values and rooted in certain moral principles. We argued that our legal system is not morally neutral and that it reflects a vision of life and an understanding of right and wrong and how it is we should live together as a nation. We substantiated this with quotes from various nonreligious bodies such as the Law Reform Commission, which wrote:

> In truth the criminal law is a moral system. It may be crude, it
> may have faults, it may be rough and ready, but basically it is
> a system of applied morality and justice. It serves to underline

those values necessary and important to society. When acts occur that seriously transgress essential values, like the sanctity of life, society must speak out and reaffirm those values. This is the true role of criminal law.

Having argued that there are certain principles that undergird our legal system, we said that it is vital that we as a nation continually examine and affirm those principles and values that give shape to, and provide grounding for, our society. We argued that the identification and interpretation of these principles is a task in which all Canadians can participate. Acknowledging that various communities in our society will bring their own perspective to bear in this discussion, we said religious communities have a unique contribution to make.

We then identified four relevant principles: the sanctity of life, the stewardship of life, the compassion for life, and communal responsibility. In each case we explained our biblical understanding of the principle and then attempted to show how this principle has been reflected in Canadian law and public policy. Thus in reference to compassion for life, we quoted from Scripture ("Love your neighbour as yourself"—Leviticus 19:18; Luke 10:27) and said the following:

> As we believe human life is created in the image of God and the object of God's love and grace, life is something that we should cherish and care for. We should love others as we love ourselves. In both the Old and New Testaments, the people of Israel and the followers of Jesus were commanded to care for the alien, the widow, the orphan, and the poor. It is this principle which is also reflected in our society's concern for the poor and the vulnerable, for those who are unable to care for themselves. It is reflected in our refugee programs and in our private and our governmental relief and development programs overseas. It is also reflected in the myriad of voluntary associations and programs that care for a variety of human needs here in Canada.

We went on to discuss the life-affirming ethos that has shaped Canadian policy in health care and, after reviewing the current law, explained how the legalization of assisted suicide or euthanasia would undermine this ethos and place vulnerable persons at risk. We also explained the implications for health care providers and the health care system. We concluded as follows:

> Euthanasia and physician assisted suicide are essentially killing those who are terminally ill or elderly. These are the very people most deserving of respect and protection in our society.

Bruce J. Clemenger

> We would strongly urge you to resist those who are calling for legalization of these forms of killing. We turn instead to an affirmation of the "death with dignity" afforded by palliative care professionals. Our concern is that the legalization of assisted suicide and euthanasia will undermine the life-affirming ethos which currently shapes our legal system. We will legitimize suicide by implying that in some situations it is acceptable. We will be saying that murder is permissible even when the victim poses no threat to anyone else. It will imply that sometimes a choice for death is legitimate and that it is sometimes permissible in our society for one person to compassionately murder another. It will suggest that life is at times optional and that our society at times sanctions the choice for death.

When we subsequently appeared before Canada's Supreme Court, our argument followed the same lines. We intervened jointly with the Canadian Conference of Catholic Bishops (CCCB) as the argument focused on the sanctity of human life, a principle to which both EFC and the CCCB subscribe. We were the only parties in the case to promote the sanctity of human life, and in a split decision, the majority grounded its decision to uphold the law on the importance of recognizing the sanctity of human life in Canadian law. Even though the law against assisted suicide was found to violate the section of the Canadian Charter of Rights and Freedoms that guarantee life, liberty, and the security of the person, the court ruled that this infringement was justified due to the state's interest in preserving the sanctity of human life.

CONCLUSION
There are several outstanding issues that still [to this day] need to be addressed. One is finding agreement on the proper role of the state. In Canada, the voting patterns of evangelicals display support for parties across the political spectrum, in numbers quite proportionate to that of the general population. While there may be consensus on the need to alleviate poverty, there is significant difference on what the role of the state should be in addressing poverty. Should the state redistribute wealth through taxation and spending on social welfare programs, or should it reduce taxes, enabling the business and private sectors to redirect their spending and provide incentives for addressing social needs through individual or corporate charitable efforts? These differences manifest themselves in support for various political approaches to the issue.

32

As James Skillen argues in his book *The Scattered Voice*, identifying the proper role of the state is a critical issue for Christian engagement.[27] Other issues that Christians grapple with are the appropriate place and influence of a dominant religion in a pluralist society; identifying appropriate limits, if any, to religious freedom and religious expression; and, as mentioned earlier, the degree of specificity that is appropriate for churches to employ in recommending policy alternatives.

The good news is that I rarely hear Christians say we should not be involved politically. If this feeling is expressed, it is more a result of frustration or exasperation than a manifestation of a view of engagement. Whereas ten years ago there was some resistance to EFC intervening before Canada's Supreme Court, it is now expected that we will intervene in the important cases. Through developing consensus on a variety of issues and articulating our perspective in a way that is acceptable to the community we represent, we are able to place new issues on the table for discussion, issues for which there is as yet no obvious point of consensus. It is a hard process, yet it forces us to confront our ideological preferences with the teaching of Scripture, which is what the renewing of our minds is all about.

PART 2

THE EMERGING PUBLIC ORTHODOXY: LIBERALISM, THE CHARTER, AND INDIVIDUAL AUTONOMY

1. INTRODUCTION

In his book *Beyond Radical Secularism*, French political philosopher Pierre Manent identified five key influences on Western societies: "The five great spiritual masses that determine the figure of the West are: Judaism, Islam, Evangelical Protestantism (mainly American), the Catholic Church and, finally, the ideology of human rights."[28] He also calls these five "spiritual forces". These five intersected at a press conference held in Toronto a few years ago.

The press conference held on January 25, 2018, focused on an interfaith letter protesting the Canada Summer Jobs attestation which organizations were required to sign to qualify for a federal government grant. The letter was signed by over ninety faith leaders, and I was one of the faith leaders at the press conference representing the first four "forces" who, in effect, rebuked the government for requiring the affirmation of an articulation of the fifth as a condition of receiving a government benefit.

The attestation reads:

> Both the job and my organization's core mandate respect individual human rights in Canada, including the values underlying the Canadian Charter of Rights and Freedoms as well as other rights. These include reproductive rights and the right to be free from discrimination on the basis of sex, religion, race, national or ethnic origin, colour, mental or physical disability or sexual orientation, or gender identity or expression.

The Liberal government expressed dismay over the refusal of many organizations to sign; they could not understand why organizations refused to check the box. They said the attestation was directed at activities that would undermine women's reproductive rights or discriminate against LGBTQ2 persons. They said their concern was with activities, and not beliefs and values. Moreover, they accused those opposing the attestation of having a political agenda.

Certainly, the flash point was the attestation's requirement that the core mandate of the organization respect reproductive rights. Those who are pro-life and who believe there should be at least some restriction on abortion in Canadian law do not oppose women's rights, but rather seek to include unborn children within the scope of human rights. We want human rights to be more inclusive. Yes, this would infringe on the unlimited freedom women currently have, but the intent is to expand the ambit of human rights, not restrict them. Some others who wished to not disclose their view on the issue felt the attestation compelled them to take sides.

Yet, the objections were broader than the issue of reproductive rights, and many editorial boards and national columnists also expressed concern for what was called a values or ideological test contained in the attestation. The attestation referenced Charter values and "other values and rights". But what specific values were being referred to? They are not listed anywhere, by Parliament or the courts. And what are the "other rights" referred to? As I said in the press conference, religious organizations have doctrinal statements at their core and take attestations seriously. How can we then be asked to respect or attest to unnamed values and un-delineated rights?

The first issue is that organizations were being required to attest to any values or beliefs as a condition of receiving the government grant. This is compelled speech and contrary to the freedoms guaranteed in sections 2a and b of the Charter. The second issue is the actual content of the attestation: expressing respect for rights, values, and the Charter. Interestingly, section 32 of the Charter states that the Charter only applies to Parliament and legislatures, and by extension any entity that is given statutory authority. It does not apply to nongovernmental actors. Is it then not strange to require an affirmation of the Charter when the purpose of the Charter is to protect individuals and nongovernmental organizations from the overreach of governments?

The attestation sought to confirm that the jobs for which funds were being sought, and the organizations that applied for funding, could attest to respecting certain rights and values. It presumed a certain meaning and interpretation of these rights and values, and presumed a priority of these over other rights and values people may hold.[29] It did not matter what else organizations believed, as long as they could attest to the specific beliefs and values selected by the government.[30]

What if the attestation read: "Both the job and my organization's core mandate respect the principles of the Bible, including values underlying the Christian faith. These include religious freedom of individuals and groups, the sanctity of human life, and the equal dignity of all persons"? This would be consistent with the preamble of the Charter, which says, "Whereas Canada was founded on the Supremacy of God and the rule of law." But then the Courts have also decided that the phrase *supremacy of God* is a "dead letter with no interpretive meaning." J. Southern of the British Columbia Court of Appeal made this declaration in the BCCA's 1999 R v. Sharpe decision. No one has seriously challenged the ability of the Court to render a part of the constitution void: that body which can set aside a part of the constitution itself becomes sovereign, as it is no longer bound by the law.

Is the attestation an expression of the ideology of human rights? If so, and if Manent is correct that this ideology in the West has the dynamic of a spiritual force, then when a set of set rights and values are used to define, promote and foster what it means to be a good Canadian, and when allegiance is demanded by governments and any dissent punished by the withholding of government benefit or protection, are we now witnessing the fermentation of a new public ideology or civil religion, a new orthodoxy to which all Canadians are expected to give allegiance? Will the new orthodoxy function as a religious or ideological test for public service as well as for receiving public benefit?

Manent, writing in the context of France, understands modern liberalism to be an orientation towards politics that is not tied to the intellectual and spiritual influence of the Catholic Church, or Christianity more generally.[31] Liberalism originated in an attempt to find a secular basis for politics. The concern was that grounding politics in a notion of a higher good or end would invite an assessment by religious standards. To avoid this, the liberal strategy is to find a basis for the political order which does not rely on any one religious tradition or vision of life but rather to find a basis acceptable to people of various faiths—it will be nonsectarian. The resulting liberalism claims to be the most accommodating political philosophy in the context of a society characterized by deep religious pluralism. It claims to be one that is neutral towards competing visions of the good and one which can provide the maximum freedom for each to pursue the good as they see it.[32]

LIBERALISM IN CANADA

In this essay, I test the proposition that liberalism as it is manifest in Canada today fulfills this promise of fairness and impartiality in a society marked by deep moral and religious diversity. After all, liberalism is the dominant political system that animates *all* of the major political parties in Canada, (Liberal Party of Canada, Conservative Party of Canada, Bloc Québécois, New Democratic Party, and The Green Party). Our political parties represent a different balancing of liberal principles, but all the parties operate out of a liberal frame. Does liberalism as it is practiced in Canada seek to treat fairly the adherents of the five spiritual forces and others? Or is liberalism in Canada becoming increasingly ideological and sectarian, manifesting the characteristics of what Manent calls a spiritual force: something ideological which promulgates an orthodoxy about the good and how to attain it, and which demands public allegiance?[33] Is there evidence that liberalism is shifting away from a nonsectarian stance and instead becoming sectarian?

I focus on the formation of law and public policy, and the principles or values used to legitimize changes to laws and policies—principles and values which citizens are assumed to affirm when acting as citizens, whichever religious or philosophical or ideological tradition they adhere to.

Politically, Canada has accepted a form of liberalism to maintain a political order that claims to accommodate deep religious, moral, and cultural differences. What is often not recognized is that many religious, moral, and cultural communities affirm the same principles that liberalism advances, principles like freedom and equality. While many presume the deep religious differences between keep them apart and require mediation, religions in Canada are quite adept at conversation and collaboration and at presenting a united front to governments.[34]

In one *Faith Today* article I wrote:

> Not only did Canada develop without a constitutional doctrine of the separation of church and state as in the United States, the Canadian constitution provided for the funding of minority religious schools: Catholic schools in predominately Protestant Ontario and Protestant schools in Catholic Quebec. Further, consider our social services sector, where Canada's largest provider besides our governments is The Salvation Army. Canada's approach has been a robust non-sectarianism, where no single set of doctrines, religious or secularist, would be imposed. At the same time, a non-sectarian approach does not presume religious neutrality or that the public square can be neutral. Rather, it recognizes that a plurality of worldviews shapes and guides the actions of citizens. The political world and the broader public realm are shaped by this doctrinal diversity. The goal is not to sanitize statecraft from this plurality, but to accommodate diversity and its expression in the fairest ways possible. In such a context, political leaders are expected to be even-handed, fair and just in their dealings with everyone.[35]

So, while advocates of liberalism claim it is neutral and nonsectarian, some contemporary expressions of Canadian liberalism show signs of embracing the promotion of certain interpretations of principles, or advancing other values, or prioritizing specific rights that not all affirm. If governments promote one of the ideologies or philosophies to which only some Canadians adhere, liberalism becomes sectarian. The more robust the sectarian doctrines it promotes, it becomes a secular equivalent to a public or civic religion, an orthodoxy to which all will be expected to accede in the public realm. A transition of this sort will take place over time, and both the nonsectarian and the sectarian impulses will be evident in different policies. It is the promulgation of the sectarian creed, the orthodoxy, in both the political and civil society that will solidify the transition. The principles are no longer merely political but are promulgated across the public sphere.

To understand this emergence, we first review the way Canada has managed religious pluralism since its founding and its subsequent transition from a Christian pluralism to a secular pluralism (chapter 2). Next, we explore if it is possible for a government to be secular and religiously neutral (chapter 3), and then we examine the nature of Canadian liberalism: how it has changed and the nature of the sectarian (sometimes called republican) variant of liberalism that is in ascendancy (chapter 4). Within the context of this emerging form of liberalism, we explore the orthodoxy being promulgated by this Canadian republicanism (liberal sectarianism) and its expression in the promotion of "Canadian values" (chapter 5). I conclude with the need to understand and challenge the new sectarian liberalism and seek ways to promote and advance (recover) a nonsectarian approach to politics (chapter 6).

I should note here that in using the term *republicanism*, I am not referring to the political ideology of the U.S. political party but rather a type of political democratic system in which a priority is placed on ensuring the acceptance and affirmation of a set of political virtues and principles which define the republic (a nation) and to which all citizens are expected to adhere regardless of their private beliefs and convictions. More than agreement on a set of procedural rules, some telltale signs of a republican system are defining the democracy in terms of specific values and the importance placed on public schooling, which is designed to inculcate and promote specific virtues deemed necessary to good citizenship. The leading example of this among Western democracies is France. As we will see, Quebec is the most "republican" of Canadian provinces, exemplified by its expectations of the public education system in inculcating civic virtues and in Bill 21.

DIRECTIONAL AND CONFESSIONAL PLURALISM
Definitions and understandings of pluralism vary. Usually, pluralism refers to the fact of diversity; that there are different religions or cultures, for example. How we respond to plurality will in part depend on the type of diversity being considered, whether diversity of food, of music, of art forms, or ethnicity and cultures, or morality and belief systems and rituals. Depending on the plurality,

some will reject some of the alternatives and some will accept all possibilities. Some will agree that all differences are good but prefer some over others, and some will go further and in a relativistic fashion suggest that all differences should be treated equally and that diversity should be encouraged, seemingly for the sake of diversity itself—to maximize choices. There are then, a plurality of ways to respond to diversity: one can seek to reduce it, be indifferent towards it, tolerate it, be resigned to it, accept it, or celebrate it. How we respond will vary depending on what plurality is the focus of our attention.

In this essay, I focus on moral and religious pluralism, or what I, following Richard Mouw and Sander Griffioen, call "directional pluralism".[36] This refers to the various religions, philosophies, belief systems, moral doctrines, or comprehensive doctrines that give direction, meaning, and purpose to people's lives (it could also be called confessional, convictional, or religious pluralism). Moral doctrines and comprehensive doctrines are the terms John Rawls uses in his book *Political Liberalism* to refer to the deep diversity of many societies. He says,

> It is comprehensive when it includes conceptions of what is of value in human life, and ideals of personal character, as well as ideals of friendship and of familial and associational relationships, and much else that is to inform our conduct, and in the limit to our life as a whole. A conception is fully comprehensive if it covers all recognized values and virtues within one rather precisely articulated system; whereas the conception is only partially comprehensive when it comprises a number of, but by no means all, nonclinical values and virtues and is rather loosely articulated.[37]

This pluralism would include utilitarianism, materialism, and atheism as well as traditional religions such as Christianity, Islam, and Judaism, and include the five spiritual forces Manent identifies. These are competing systems of doctrines and practices (their respective claims are universal) and, in many aspects and conclusions, are contradictory and cannot be reconciled. When more than one of these has adherents within the same society, this is a condition of deep pluralism, a condition which does not lend itself to indifference due to the deep differences between citizens.

In this context, toleration is often misunderstood. To tolerate is premised on disagreement; it means you choose not to restrict an activity or belief you disagree with when you have the ability to do so.[38] This is not the same as indifference, which means you don't care, or resignation, which means you may not like it but cannot do anything about it.[39]

Some think "mere" tolerance is too low of a bar. But there is nothing "mere" about tolerance.[40] It is critical to living with religious differences where the core beliefs of one may be heresy, blasphemy, or nonsense to others. As a Christian, I affirm all people are created in the image of God and thereby have dignity. So, I respect each person's God-given freedom to pursue truth and exercise their consciences.[41] I may not always agree with their conclusions or the ways of life that flow from their beliefs and commitments—what philosophers sometimes refer to as their "conception of the good". But I can tolerate much out of respect for God's intent and the dignity of each as they exercise the free will God gave us all. To tolerate does not mean I abandon my beliefs, but rather toleration is an expression of my beliefs.

The limits a society places on tolerance are set out in codes of behaviour like a criminal code or human rights codes, which identify activities that are not deemed acceptable, and for which one is punished. Politics is a process by which we decide what is and what is not acceptable behaviour—and, within the sphere of the permissible, politics is also the art of managing differences and entails forming a functional political community among citizens who believe differently. Some idea of public justice will guide the political community in adjudicating and harmonizing the various claims of the plurality of institutions and associations that contextualize directional differences. As Hannah Arendt wrote, "Politics is based on the fact of human plurality ... From the very start, politics organizes those who are absolutely different with a view to their relative equality and in contradistinction to their relative differences."[42] Is it possible to find agreement on how we can live together and maintain political and legal order while respecting these deep differences and not be marginalized by the state for our beliefs and the practices that flow from them?

2. THE SUCCESSIVE DIRECTIONAL PLURALISMS OF CANADA

At the time of the establishment of Canada, directional pluralism included the predominant Christian traditions along with a variety of indigenous forms of spirituality (which were given little significance in the political order of that time). Other faiths had few adherents.[43]

Until the 1970s, historian George W. Egerton says, Christianity through its national denominations was the only religion having public functions: "most specifically on the dialectic of religion and politics in both formal and informal constitutional discourse, as Canadians attempted to identify and legislate the fundamental principles, values, rights, institutions, and procedures by which they wish to be governed."[44] In this way Christianity served as the public faith.

Egerton identifies three successive pluralisms that shaped Canadian jurisprudence and politics since Confederation, and he tells the story of the transitioning from a "self-proclaimed 'Christian democracy' of denominational or Christian pluralism, through an interval of religious pluralism, to a secularist pluralism based on the way the courts and politicians have applied the charter."[45] With this unfolding history in mind, I focus on the relationship of the public faith of Christianity in the recognition and formalizing of human rights in Canadian law, and what is replacing Christianity as the animator of our current public faith.

CHRISTIAN PLURALISM

From its inception, Canada was dominated by Christian pluralism. Though Canada had no official state church, Christian denominations provided the moral and spiritual glue for Canadian society. Historian John Webster Grant writes:

> Unlike the United States, which imbibed a tradition of secularism from its founding fathers, Canada grew up under the tutelage of its churches. The pulpit, the school and the press were the leading forces in molding the Canadian character. Almost all the well-known educators of the period were clergymen, and many leading newspapers were in effect organs of particular religious groups ... By preaching, editorializing, and founding universities, they sought on the one hand to lay the moral and spiritual foundations of nationhood, and on the other, to act as a conscience to the state.[46]

Canadian churches, says Grant, shared the "conviction that in the main the institutions and values of Western society rested on a Christian foundation."[47] In contrast to the establishment of national churches in Europe,

> Colonial legislatures determined by the time of Confederation that no church or churches should receive such official recognition in Canada. The purpose of this arrangement, however, was not to deny the nation's allegiance to the Christian god but merely to allow equal opportunities for all denominations. The status of Canada as a Christian nation was never in question, and in practice the churches were regarded more as public than private institutions. This belief in the existence of Christendom and in Canada's place within it was a common presupposition that made possible mutual understanding and occasionally even collaboration among Christians of various denominations ... Canada required the active participation of [the] churches if it were to be viable as a nation, and equally the churches required a strong Canada if they were not to lose the most promising young people to the United States.[48]

Without a formal national church, in Canada a plurality of Christian denominations functioned as the unofficial state church. While Christendom faded in Europe after the Second World War, it took a few decades longer in Canada. Grant says that

> the assumption that the Christian faith provides recognized values of Western society [have] been increasingly questioned in Europe since the enlightenment of the 18th century, and indeed ever since the end of the Middle Ages ... After the Second World War and the Chinese Revolution no one believed in Christendom longer, or any rate no one outside North America.[49]

It is important to note that while the churches sought to shape the character and direction of Canada, these efforts were not expressed in religiously aligned political parties. Catholics and Protestants found their political homes in secular political parties that were formed around basic orientations to law and policy without explicit connections to any one specific Christian tradition, let alone Christianity. Perhaps the connections were assumed, and certainly politicians had strong personal links to the various Christian traditions manifest in Canada. When some felt that the two main parties, the Liberals and Conservatives, were mishandling the welfare of the nation, two movements emerged that were in part animated by distinct Christian principles but were framed as populist responses and not as religious or sectarian parties. The pursuit of the social gospel found expression in the Co-operative Commonwealth Federation, later the New Democratic Party.[50]

Meanwhile the Social Credit party was founded by more conservative Christian impulses and the roots of the Reform Party can be traced back to the Social Credit. Neither identified their political movements in explicitly Christian terms though the leaders of both "Bible Bill" Aberhart, a Bible college president and radio preacher, and J.S. Woodsworth, a Methodist pastor, were animated by a strong and passionate Christian faith yet sought to manifest this in a secular expression.

THE DEMISE OF CHRISTENDOM IN CANADA

Grant, Egerton, and other Canadian historians such as Margarite Van Die locate the time of the demise of this political influence of Christianity in the 1960s. Notably,

> Canadians were shielded from the full impact of the assault on Christendom by their lingering pluralism and isolationism, and they did not immediately recognize the signs that warned of its decline ... Realization that Christendom was dead, even in Canada, dawned with surprising suddenness in the 1960s.[51]

Van Die describes the celebration on Parliament Hill on July 1, 1967, and the degree to which expressions of the Christian faith were present in the ceremony (Bible readings, hymns sung, and the refrain repeated by all—"We dedicate ourselves to you, O Lord").[52] She uses the language of "shadow establishments" to describe the influence of the Roman Catholic Church in Quebec and Protestant denominations in English-speaking Canada. Yet she and others say the decline was already in process by the 1960s. Grant concluded, "The unofficial establishment of Christianity in Canada, already in 1967 more shadow and substance, is in 1987 little more than a memory."[53]

Within this period of Christian pluralism, the shadow establishments of Christian churches functioned sociologically as the civil religion that shaped public rituals, symbols, and ceremonies and was the dominant influence on the moral foundations of Canada. They provided either formally or informally the priestly functions of legitimizing government authority, serving as chaplain to public institutions, and upholding public morality; the pastoral function of providing social services; and the prophetic function of engaging in moral crusades (temperance, prohibition, Lord's Day observance, laws against vices) and engaging in debates over public values and behavior.[54]

Egerton says that the political rhetoric portraying Canada as a Christian state continued after the Second World War as churches geographically "occupied a central place in public space" (alongside banks and government buildings) and "served as centers for social and cultural activities of communities, besides their specifically religious activities," Church leaders would claim that the churches speak as the "conscience of the state."[55]

In terms of the influence of this Christian hegemony's influence on law, an illustration is the formulation and acceptance of human rights documents.[56] In the development of the *Universal Declaration of Human Rights* and subsequently the *Canadian Bill of Rights*, Egerton writes:

> Religious teachings touch directly on human rights campaigns, both supportively and critically and, from an early point in the project for the Universal Declaration, Canadian churches played a vital national and international role in shaping opinion, articulating political values, and influencing policy, even as Canadian civil libertarian initiatives often came from the more secularist forces of labor and the political left. Canadian religion functioned ambiguously—progressively and prophetically on the one hand, joining with liberal and secularist proponents of the Canadian Bill of Rights to re-envision Canadian political culture, and conservatively on the other, to legitimate governmental authority as part of the churches' traditional priestly role in defining the nation's moral and legal norms and guarding the state against external and internal dangers. While Canadian national churches advocated protection of human rights, as in the United Church's Report on Church, Nation and World Order, their support was conditioned upon such rights being give given an explicit theological foundation which reflected the traditional fusion of Christian and democratic values in Canadian history.[57]

Canada at first hesitated to sign the Universal Declaration when a theological premise was not included, though it eventually did sign at the urging of Lester B. Pearson (who later became the leader of the Liberal Party and Prime Minister), who was at that time the head of the Canadian delegation.

The issue of a theological premise returned in the process of drafting the Canadian Bill of Rights guided by Conservative Prime Minister John

Diefenbaker. In its report, the Senate committee affirmed a transcendent ground for human rights, stating, "Such rights are not treated by men, be they ever so numerous, for the benefit of other men, nor are they the gift of governments. They are above the power of men to create."[58] Pressure to include a theological premise was advocated by church leaders as well as politicians. Egerton notes the report portrayed Canada as a "Christian country" and recommended "that all men give thought to the Fatherhood of God and the Brotherhood of Man." [59] He says this blending of Christianity and liberalism would continue through the 1950s. The Bill of Rights was passed in 1960, its preamble stating:

> The Parliament of Canada, affirming that the Canadian nation is founded upon principles that acknowledge the supremacy of God, the dignity and worth of the human person and the position of the family in a society and of free men and free institutions; affirming also that men and institutions remain free only when freedom is founded upon respect for moral and spiritual values and the rule of law.

However, the challenge to the Christian hegemony was, says Egerton,

> generated by constitutional debates and decisions, and especially the centrally important quest to define and constitutionally entrench human rights, illuminate most clearly the historic shifting and the relations of religion and politics, church and state, in Canada's political culture, where the former public functions of churches were challenged and displaced with the secularist liberal ideology and jurisprudence.[60]

In this shift we see the emerging influence of what Manent calls the ideology of human rights, one of the five spiritual forces he identifies, and which Egerton says eventually replaced Christian pluralism.

TRANSITIONAL RELIGIOUS PLURALISM

During the debates over the Bill of Rights, the Jewish community was consulted to ensure that the preamble would not cause offense. This sensitivity, says Egerton, marked the transition from a Christian pluralism to a religious pluralism, even though "Christianity remained privileged in Canadian constitutional law and public rituals."[61] However, other religious communities and indigenous leaders were not formally consulted.

The public function and influence of churches on politics was weakening, a symbol of this change being a new national flag bearing no Christian symbol.

Bruce J. Clemenger

While the participation of religions in the national life of Canada was still encouraged in the 1960s, notably in the centennial celebrations and Expo '67, the Royal Commission on Bilingualism and Biculturalism conducted a multi-year examination of Canadian nationhood and ultimately defined Canada in terms of culture and language, and not religion. As Egerton writes:

> With the displacement of religion from its former partnership with liberal ideology in defining national identity, by the late 1960s Canada was on the verge of several decades of radical re-imaginings which would witness transformative change in its constitution, jurisprudence and, not least, [in] the public functions of religion. Indeed, the defining elements of Canadian pluralism would shift from religion to language and ethnicity, as multiculturalism supplanted biculturalism in a new quest for national identity, purpose and unity. Simultaneously, Canada legislators embraced the protection of human rights as the fundamental legitimator of renewed government authority and purpose, as human rights commissions and tribunals would soon proliferate nationally and provincially. By the time that religious questions would return to the renewed Canadian constitutional discourse directed by Pierre Trudeau as justice minister and then prime minister after 1968, Canadian public life and rhetoric would be in process of rapid de-Christianization, while jurisprudence and social theory were searching for new, nonreligious foundations ...
>
> It was the genius of Trudeau's politics to project updated themes of classical liberal ideology, brilliantly indigenized for Canadian appeal: federalism and bilingualism to confront the separatists after aspirations of Quebec nationalism; multicultural pluralism to accommodate in and contain ethnic assertion and ideological conflict; civil libertarianism to enshrine protection for individual rights and counter "tribalism" in a revised constitution; participatory democracy to expand citizenship in shaping a just society; and secularism to disentangle a modernized Canadian legal order from ... traditional religious norms and constraints.[62]

SECULAR PLURALISM

Egerton says the "project to modernize Canadian law and liberate it from its religious framework" began with divorce legislation in 1967. At that time, then justice minister Pierre Elliot Trudeau of the Liberal Party who would soon become prime minister said in a speech to the House of Commons:

> We are now living in a social climate in which people are beginning to realize, perhaps for the first time in the history of this country, that we are not entitled to impose the concepts which belong to a sacred society upon a civil or profane society. The concepts of the civil society in which we live are pluralistic, and I think this parliament realizes that it would be a mistake for us to try to legislate into the society concepts which belong to a theological or sacred order.[63]

Trudeau also initiated legislation dealing with other issues such as lotteries, birth control, homosexuality, and abortion, and these were combined in an Omnibus Bill that was passed in 1969, when Trudeau was prime minister.

The referent points for Canadian law and politics were changing:

> The decades of the 1960s to 1980s were transformative in the history of the Canadian state and in the history of Canadian churches and in the relationship of these institutions. The change in relationships saw the churches lose most of their former public functions, priestly and pastoral roles, as religion was differentiated in political culture and privatized in civil society.[64]

The debates over the wording of the Charter of Rights and Freedoms (Charter) in 1980 and 1981 included controversy over what language would be used to express the foundation of the freedoms and rights that would be guaranteed. Would the language of the Charter be secular and suggest rights and freedoms are human artifice and conferred by government by the will of citizens, are they inherent or unique to human beings, or do rights originate in that which transcends human convention and humanity itself, being rooted in the dignity we enjoy by virtue of our being created in the image of God?

Evangelicals and Catholics pressed for the inclusion of a theological premise in the preamble of the Charter, although Trudeau said, "It was strange, so long after the Middle Ages that some politicians felt obliged to mention God in a constitution which is, after all, a secular and not a spiritual document." In the end, he conceded to its inclusion though he said privately to the Liberal caucus he did not think "God gives a damn whether he was in the constitution or not."[65]

In pressing for the inclusion of an affirmation that human rights are not simply of human artifice, The Evangelical Fellowship of Canada argued:

> The acknowledgment of one Supreme God to whom we as a nation are answerable gives ground for legislation bearing on all matters human. To omit any such reference only leaves the door open for substitution of other less worthy grounds—utilitarianism, naturalism, secularism, etc.—since legislation cannot escape growing out of presuppositions. Moreover, human rights though recognized by the state in the democratic society are a sacred endowment from God, not bestowed but administered by the state.[66]

The contention of the EFC was that legislation generally, and the idea of human rights specifically, will be rooted in some system of belief or philosophy. If not belief in God in whose image we are created, the source of our dignity and worth, then in a substitute.

While reference to the supremacy of God was included in the preamble of the Charter, Egerton says that this was a temporary reprieve from the more complete transition to a secularist pluralism which seeks nonreligious foundations for jurisprudence and legislation. Egerton writes:

> The constitutional reference to God, however, did not mean that the deeper cultural political tides of privatizing religion have been reversed or that the traditional public functions of religion in Canadian political history had been restored. The constitutional reference had come as a result of tactical political calculations, not from any conversion on the part of Trudeau or the Liberals to the philosophical or theological convictions expressed by Conservative leaders, let alone by The Evangelical Fellowship of Canada. If Trudeau's desire to remove theology from politics suffered a temporary reverse, the Charter itself would serve to launch a new era of secularist pluralism in Canadian jurisprudence. Indeed, similar to the patterns of jurisprudence through the post 1960s decades in Britain and United States, the Canadian church-state relationship would be transformed as a Christian religion would see the state largely divest itself of religion's traditional priestly functions

of legitimating government authority and law, and its pastoral functions in guarding family and sexual morality.[67]

Some branches of Christianity continued to engage politically. Egerton says that as in the U.S., "It has been the evangelical Protestants and Catholics, together with leaders from Judaism and other world religions, who from the 1980s have resisted most determinedly the exclusion of public religion by the courts and legislatures of Canada and have mobilized politically to regain voices in the public square." He notes that Prime Ministers Brian Mulroney (Conservative) and Jean Chrétien (Liberal) remained inattentive or hostile to public religion and that "the Canadian pattern of secularization will continue to resemble more the European experience."[68]

It was the Charter and its application that solidified the transition from a Christian pluralism through a religious pluralism to a secularist one:

> It has been the courts, interpreting the 1982 Canadian Charter of Rights and Freedoms, which have largely supplanted the churches as "the conscience of the state," as Canada has evolved from its traditional Christian pluralism, through the religious pluralism of the 1950s and the Confederation centenary, to the secularist pluralism that now exercises liberal ideological hegemony in the country's political culture.[69]

Egerton concludes that with the inclusion of the Charter in the constitution, the liberal ideological hegemony had replaced the Christian hegemony.

Note the language used by Egerton: "secularist" and "liberal ideological hegemony". While Egerton uses the term *secularist*, there are variants of secularism that describe the state's engagement with religion. I focus on two—what I label *secular* is the nonsectarian approach where states treat all belief systems or comprehensive doctrines with fairness. In contrast, a *secularist* approach entails attempts by the state to privatize religious expression and ground law and public policy in a sectarian secular ideology. Egerton in using this latter term *secularist* anticipates the transition to the second and less accommodating approach to religion by states. Liberalism has claimed to be neutral and nonsectarian in how it manages the directional pluralism of a given society. And for some liberals, this is their intent. Egerton, however, is identifying the emergence of a sectarian form of liberalism, what I call liberal sectarianism. I spoke into this reality in 2008: "The challenges we face to societal norms ... come ... from the unfolding of liberalism and its secularist expression, very much a western ideology birthed out of Christendom."[70]

Bruce J. Clemenger

Next, we explore the nature of the secularism that regulates the Canadian political order and its claim to be neutral amidst directional pluralism before turning to an examination of the ideological turn of Canadian liberalism.

3. CHANGING CANADIAN SECULARISM

To better appreciate the shift in the past few decades, it is important to understand the nature of religious freedom as referred to in the Charter, and then the ideas emerging after several key court case interventions. By 2017, religious freedom needed a simple reiteration:

> Religious freedom is specifically mentioned in Canada's Charter of Rights and Freedoms because it refers to a distinct dimension of life. Its importance is widely recognized and deemed necessary to guarantee in laws worldwide. The Charter also guarantees freedom of conscience, thought, belief and opinion, plus expression—freedom of the press, of peaceful assembly, of association. These other freedoms would cover most of the activities of a church, but religion is specifically mentioned because there is something unique about religious freedom, which includes the communal expression of faith in something that transcends and to which we are bound.[71]

Let us consider the shift.

THE SHIFT TO SECULARISM

The first case in which religious freedom was adjudicated by Canada's Supreme Court under the Charter was the Big M Drug Mart case in 1985. The case challenged the Lord's Day Act which required most stores to be closed on Sundays. Chief Justice Brian Dixon, writing for the majority, argued that under the Charter laws need to have a secular and not a religious purpose. He wrote:

> It is recognized that for a great number of Canadians, Sunday is the day when their souls rest in God, when the spiritual takes priority over the material, a day which, to them, gives security and meaning because it is linked to Creation and the Creator. It is a day which brings a balanced perspective to life, an opportunity for man to be in communion with man and with God. In my view, however, as I read the Charter, it mandates that the legislative preservation of a Sunday day of rest should be secular, the diversity of belief and non-belief, the diverse socio-cultural backgrounds of Canadians make it constitutionally incompetent for the federal

Parliament to provide legislative preference for any one religion at
the expense of those of another religious persuasion.[72]

This principled shift to secularism, that law and public policy not be sectarian,
that is, justified by appeal to any one set of beliefs, was reaffirmed in subsequent
decisions of the court.

In the1993 Rodriguez case on assisted suicide, the intervening Evangelical
Fellowship of Canada and Canadian Conference of Catholic Bishops argued
that the issue of euthanasia raises deep theological and philosophical issues and
concerns the very meaning of the sanctity of human life which the interveners
said was an underlying norm of Canadian society.[73] Then Chief Justice Lamer
wanted to view the issue more narrowly.[74] In his dissenting opinion, he wrote:

> Can the right to choose at issue here, that is the right to choose
> suicide, be described as an advantage of which the appellant is
> being deprived? In my opinion, the Court should answer this
> question without reference to the philosophical and theological
> considerations fuelling the debate on the morality of suicide or
> euthanasia. It should consider the question before it from a legal
> perspective—Tremblay v. Daigle, [1989] 2 S.C.R. 530—while
> keeping in mind that the Charter has established the essentially
> secular nature of Canadian society and the central place of
> freedom of conscience in the operation of our institutions.[75]

The other judges in the case also affirmed the secular nature of Canadian
society; however, the majority did not believe this precluded them from considering
the broader issues involved in the issue of assisted suicide. The majority anchored
its decision on the principle of the sanctity of human life that the interveners
championed, though the court said they meant it in the secular sense—the
affirmation of the sanctity of human life being shared by many different worldviews.
The majority (five of nine) agreed that the prohibition on assisted suicide was
necessary to protect the sanctity of human life. This shifted in the 9-0 Carter
decision rendered in 2015 where the Court ruled that in some circumstances
individual autonomy would outweigh the ban on assisted suicide.

As Justice Dickson said in Big M, "A truly free society is one which can
accommodate a wide variety of beliefs, diversity of tastes and pursuits, customs
and codes of conduct." He wrote,

> The essence of the concept of freedom of religion is the right to
> entertain such religious beliefs as a person chooses, the right to
> declare religious beliefs openly and without fear of hindrance or

reprisal, and the right to manifest religious belief by worship and practice or by teaching and dissemination. But the concept means more than that.

Freedom can primarily be characterized by the absence of coercion or constraint. If a person is compelled by the state or the will of another to a course of action or inaction which he would not otherwise have chosen, he is not acting of his own volition and he cannot be said to be truly free. One of the major purposes of the Charter is to protect, within reason, from compulsion or restraint. Coercion includes not only such blatant forms of compulsion as direct commands to act or refrain from acting on pain of sanction; coercion includes indirect forms of control which determine or limit alternative courses of conduct available to others. Freedom in a broad sense embraces both the absence of coercion and constraint, and the right to manifest beliefs and practices. Freedom means that, subject to such limitations as are necessary to protect public safety, order, health, or morals or the fundamental rights and freedoms of others, no one is to be forced to act in a way contrary to his beliefs or his conscience.

What may appear good and true to a majoritarian religious group, or to the state acting at their behest, may not, for religious reasons, be imposed upon citizens who take a contrary view. The Charter safeguards religious minorities from the threat of "the tyranny of the majority."[76]

The limitation on freedom is identified as that which is necessary to protect "public safety, order, health, or morals." Section 1 of the Charter allows the freedoms and rights listed in the Charter to be infringed if doing so is justifiable in a free and democratic society, and in this decision Justice Dickson suggests the grounds upon which restrictions would be justifiable. In this essay, my focus is on the issue of morals and limitations on freedoms that might be justified by a promotion of Charter values.

In part, the secular nature of Canadian society is understood to mean that law or public policy cannot be based in any one sectarian view, or impose or favour a specific comprehensive doctrine, or have a sectarian purpose. Laws and policies must be nonsectarian and accommodate a variety of beliefs. This is no simple task if we take these disagreements seriously and understand the depth of disagreement that exists. How can we find agreement on matters like genetic technologies, prostitution, euthanasia, the content of public education, what forms and content of speech are tolerable, and how governments should regulate the economy? Our understanding of issues such as these is rooted in our respective understandings of the very meaning and purpose of life and of human dignity. In cases like prostitution or euthanasia, for example, a government not taking a position is necessarily opting for decriminalization.[77] If the government provides public education, it must decide the content.

This meaning of being secular is expressed in the idea of the state being nonsectarian. It envisions a political order that is unbiased and accommodates deep directional diversity—a wide variety of ways of life, each grounded in differing comprehensive doctrines. While not privileging one over another, in managing diversity and providing political order, the state will seek to follow principles that are common to, and shared by, adherents of the various doctrines. It will seek to be "neutral" or impartial towards the various doctrines and beliefs to which Canadians adhere.

As we see later, any given political order will be influenced by some set of principles and procedures that will shape the laws and policies of the state—what I call the political creed. The state cannot be completely "neutral". The political task is to find a grounding for these principles and a rationale for the procedures which is compatible with the directional diversity of the citizenry. This was the issue with the Lord's Day Act. It was consistent with the Christian hegemony but remained sectarian as it was grounded in a theological premise.

As Justice Dickson said, laws and policies cannot be based on any one sectarian view. They must find adherence by people who affirm a variety of comprehensive doctrines or ideologies. A law that closed stores on Sunday based on the premise of the benefits of a common pause day would likely be found to be constitutional, and both religious and secular arguments could be advanced to justify it. British philosopher John Gray calls this convergence liberalism. The principles and procedures that shape law and public policy are the product of a convergence among the comprehensive doctrines adhered to by citizens, policies which can be justified by appealing to those various doctrines.[78]

Historically, the constitution of Canada and its legislatures needed to recognize and function within the context of the predominantly Catholic and Protestant populations and the prevalent linguistic duality. Before Confederation religious diversity was accommodated in the 1774 Quebec Act of the British Parliament which removed an oath to the British monarch and guaranteed the free practice of the Roman Catholic faith, meaning that a Roman Catholic could hold public office.

The accommodation of the religious duality was necessary to the establishment of Canada given its demographics. The British North America

Act, 1867, contained no religious premise.[79] It was, in effect, a contract between four provinces laying out their individual responsibilities and what would be the responsibilities of the federal government. It was framed in such a way that people of different faiths could accept. As historian John Webster Grant described it:

> Confederation was an offspring of secular statesmanship, born of political and economic necessity, fathered by politicians and railway promoters. Its purpose was not to create a covenant people or hasten the coming of the kingdom of God but to ensure continued British presence in North America that would be strong enough to withstand powerful pressures towards continental consolidation. Church assemblies saw no need to comment on the debates that led up to it, regarding it as a project that lay outside their terms of reference. Canadians have always recognized the secular origins of their nation. Unlike many citizens of the United States, they have never been disposed to regard their national constitutional as a quasi-religious document. The story of Confederation can be told, and indeed sometimes has been told, without reference to the church.[80]

The Christian hegemony in Canada provided the background culture within which the constitution was negotiated, and the courts and legislatures operated. In the political order, the state would be secular in that the constitution, laws, and government policies would not be rooted in any one sectarian doctrine but would be fair and impartial in the articulation and justification of the guiding principles and procedures within the broader Christian hegemony. Over time, the Christian hegemony eroded. As Canada became more directionally diverse, advocates for other views became more politically engaged and the influence of Christian denominations became less unified in their political advocacy.[81] The challenge was to find principles and procedures that are sustainable within a society marked by deep diversity without being sectarian.

NEUTRAL?
The terms usually used to denote this approach to directional pluralism in the political realm are *neutral* and *secular*. The state is to be fair and unbiased in its treatment of the various comprehensive doctrines to which citizens adhere (neutral) and does not justify any of its laws or policies in terms of any one comprehensive doctrine (secular). As presented in the next section, this nonsectarian character of being secular was originally framed with the presumption that *sect* referred to

a religion. More recently, this has been expanded to include ideologies as well as religions.

The idea of state neutrality, however, requires some examination. As in all debates key founding principles and their interpretation are at stake, and one court decision does not a guarantee make. Regarding the idea of neutrality,

> In Canada there has historically not been a barrier to government funding for programs of faith-based organizations … these issues are not just about accreditation of a law school or job grant. They are about what it means to live in a liberal democracy and how governments treat us—particularly those with minority views, the dissenters and non-conformists.[82]

The accommodation of dissenters is a core challenge; "how to treat minorities is an old debate, to which the political tradition in Western Europe and North America of liberalism was intended to be a solution." How this is accomplished is shifting.

The original expression of liberalism historically in Canada was non-sectarian. "Liberalism said: No religious tests. Governments are non-sectarian. All can fully participate and benefit from government programs and fully participate in the society."[83] However, this has shifted; "How ironic that a tradition which historically rejected religious tests is now dabbling in values tests, which have exactly the same effect!" It is important to remember that

> The Charter is intended to facilitate and protect our ability to pursue our respective conceptions of the good life with minimal interference from the government. As is often said: it is to be a shield (to protect minorities) and not a sword (to force them to adopt majority values) … If the current trend away from a fairness model of neutrality continues, we can only anticipate more attestations being required for organizations to receive different government benefits, and more attempts to require conformity to an undefined and changeable set of Charter values.[84]

All this begs the question whether such neutrality is even possible, let alone a guaranteed commodity in state affairs. While the philosophical impossibility of neutrality can be acknowledged in one decision,[85] it can just as easily be disregarded or eclipsed in another. This process goes to the heart of why it is important to intervene in the Courts and before Parliament and on an ongoing basis (as witnessing to an alternative set of principles).

For example, the decision not to regulate prostitution is not neutral but is taking sides on a contentious issue. Law and government policy will be based on some set of principles. It will have a political creed.

Justice Deschamps of the Supreme Court of Canada, writing for the majority in a case involving education about religion, acknowledged the impossibility of absolute state neutrality:

> We must also accept that, from a philosophical standpoint, absolute neutrality does not exist ... Therefore, following a realistic and non-absolutist approach, state neutrality is assured when the state neither favours nor hinders any particular religious belief, that is, when it shows respect for all postures towards religion, including that of having no religious beliefs whatsoever, while taking into account the competing constitutional rights of the individuals affected.[86]

The "realistic and non-absolutist approach" will be based on some principles likely shared by one or more comprehensive doctrines. While it may claim to be neutral in that it is indifferent to various "postures", philosophically it cannot be directionally neutral.

How impartial, then, can it be? Is it merely a procedural approach to providing a fair political order within a directionally plural society, as is often claimed, or is it itself a manifestation of one of the moral or religious systems? Will a secularist approach to managing directional pluralism be more fair or impartial than another approach? In her decision, Justice Deschamps quoted Richard Moon to explain the challenge of neutrality:

> If secularism or agnosticism constitutes a position, worldview, or cultural identity equivalent to religious adherence, then its proponents may feel excluded or marginalized when the state supports even the most ecumenical religious practices. But by the same token, the complete removal of religion from the public sphere may be experienced by religious adherents as the exclusion of their worldview and the affirmation of a non-religious or secular perspective ...
>
> Ironically, then, as the exclusion of religion from public life, in the name of religious freedom and equality, has become more complete, the secular has begun to appear less neutral and more partisan. With the growth of agnosticism and atheism, religious neutrality in the public sphere may have become impossible.

> What for some is the neutral ground on which freedom of religion and conscience depends is for others a partisan anti-spiritual perspective.[87]

Neutrality can mean an approach that is fair and impartial in its dealings with all comprehensive doctrines that engage in the public sphere (neutrality as fairness), or it can mean that it avoids religious comprehensive doctrines and only recognizes secular ones (neutrality as non-religious). Secular can mean the state does not justify its policies on any one comprehensive doctrine (nonsectarian) or that it bases its decisions on only secular ideologies (secularist).

As noted in the next section, this nonsectarian approach was originally framed with the presumption that *sect* referred to a religion. More recently, this has been expanded to include ideologies as well as religions. Justifying policies on a specific religious comprehensive doctrine would be religious sectarianism.

SECULAR AS NONSECTARIAN

Historically in Canada, the meaning of being a secular state meant that the state would be nonsectarian. It would give no privilege to any one sect, while recognizing the role comprehensive doctrines, notably Christian ones, play in the public life of Canada. Due to the predominance of Christianity and the public influence of its large denominations, it sought to be nonsectarian in not privileging a specific denomination; Canada did not have a state church. As other religious traditions gained adherence and as secular ideologies became more prominent—that is, as the number of sects increased—the scope of the nonsectarian approach widened.

In the Chamberlin case, Justice Gonthier rejected the idea that secular means nonreligious and affirmed that secular means nonsectarian, and that sects include atheistic systems of belief. Rejecting the interpretation that secular means nonreligious, he wrote,

> This is incorrect since nothing in the Charter, political or democratic theory, or a proper understanding of pluralism demands that atheistically based moral positions trump religiously based moral positions on matters of public policy.[88]

He rejects the idea that "if one's moral view manifests from a religiously grounded faith, it is not to be heard in the public square, but if it does not, then it is publicly acceptable."

He continues:

> The problem with this approach is that everyone has "belief" or "faith" in something, be it atheistic, agnostic or religious.

To construe the "secular" as the realm of the "unbelief" is therefore erroneous. Given this, why, then, should the religiously informed conscience be placed at a public disadvantage or disqualification? To do so would be to distort liberal principles in an illiberal fashion and would provide only a feeble notion of pluralism. The key is that people will disagree about important issues, and such disagreement, where it does not imperil community living, must be capable of being accommodated at the core of a modern pluralism.[89]

In short, we are all believers.[90] In this understanding secular and nonsectarian does not mean the absence or irrelevance of religion (for the state or for the citizen), but rather the equal treatment of all beliefs and traditions—religious and secular—i.e. what I have been calling comprehensive doctrines.

As I wrote in a *Faith Today* column:

A secular society, the way the courts are interpreting it, respects and accommodates religious differences. In this understanding, being secular means being nonsectarian. It is a way of managing religious diversity while being guided by public principles that all can affirm from their respective set of beliefs. Government bodies violate their mandate when they require religious communities to be themselves secular and adopt secular values.[91]

Canadian philosophers Jocelyn Maclure and Charles Taylor are advocates of this approach. In a society marked by directional pluralism, or what Maclure and Taylor, following Isaiah Berlin, call moral pluralism ("the phenomenon of individuals adopting sometimes incompatible values systems and conceptions of the good"[92]), secularism emphasizes the impartiality and nonsectarianism of the state. Maclure and Taylor affirm this interpretation of *secular*:

The establishment of a strong organic link between the state and one religion, as in the tradition of Christendom, would make members of other religions and of those professing no religion into second-class citizens. The democratic state must therefore be neutral or impartial in its relations with different faiths. It must also treat equally citizens who act on religious beliefs and those who do not; it must, in other words, be neutral in relation to the different worldviews and conceptions of the good—secular, spiritual, and religious—with which citizens identify.[93]

Being neutral means the state must not pick favourites.

> In a society where there is no consensus about religious and philosophical outlooks, however, the state must avoid hierarchizing the conceptions of the good life that form the basis of citizens' adherence to the basic principles of their political association. In the realm of core beliefs and commitments, the state, to be truly everyone's state, must remain neutral.[94]

It means embracing a "position of neutrality not only towards religion but also towards the different philosophical conceptions that stand as the secular equivalents of religion." Here we encounter the dual meaning of the term *secular*: it can mean not being grounded in any one doctrine and fair to all, or it can mean finding a completely areligious foundation and set of principles—a moral system that is an equivalent to religion. Maclure and Taylor write:

> In fact, a political system that replaces religion with a comprehensive secular philosophy as a foundation of its actions makes all the faithful members of religion into second-class citizens, since these citizens do not embrace the reasons and evaluations enshrined in the officially recognized philosophy. In other words, the political system replaces established religion, as well as the core beliefs that define it, with the secular but anti-religious moral philosophy, which in turn establishes an order of metaphysical and moral beliefs.[95]

The problem is, as we have seen above, the state cannot be completely neutral or nonsectarian, as not all views will be treated equally as Justice Deschamps and Moon point out. If there is no neutral ground, then any basis by which the state will try to be impartial while justifying its policies on some set of principles will seem biased to some.

As we have seen, the historic Canadian approach interprets secular neutrality as meaning nonsectarian and fair: the government does not play favourites, treats all the same, and justifies its policy decisions in reasons accessible to as many as possible. As I suggested previously, in attempting to be fair and nonsectarian, it must be aware that its political creed has been shaped by the dominant comprehensive doctrines, and the resulting laws, policies, and institutions may have created an uneven playing field for adherents of other comprehensive doctrines.

For example, when staff of a number of evangelical ministries had their claims for clergy housing allowances challenged by the Canadian Revenue

Agency, it become clear that the template the government used to determine the nature of a religious order and hence who would be considered a member of the clergy was based on Roman Catholic orders. The more like a Catholic order an evangelical ministry and its staff appeared, the more likely they were to be allowed the deduction. I don't think there was an intentional bias against evangelical ministries. Rather the developers of the template were likely most familiar with Roman Catholic parishes and religious orders, and their characteristics (such as vows of poverty) were used to develop the template. The legal challenges forced an evaluation of the template to ensure it was not biased towards any one faith group.

As the state cannot be completely neutral, the state and citizens should be aware of the influence of the prevailing comprehensive doctrines and culture that shaped the political creed and public institutions and their practices, and work to ensure the effects are minimal while seeking to accommodate all. Sometimes the courts are the avenue used to press the case for fairness and accommodation.

Hence in government funding decisions or when governments partner with nongovernmental organizations, the government is to act with indifference to whatever faith animates the group they are working with. The focus is properly on the activities being funded, which should of course be ones that contribute to the public good. Thus, in Canada historically there has not been a barrier to government funding for programs of faith-based organizations. The Salvation Army, a Christian denomination, is the largest nongovernmental social service provider in Canada and receives a considerable amount of its funding from various levels of government. In the case of the Canada Summer Jobs grants, the funding should not be contingent on attesting to some set of values but on whether the job being subsidized meets the employment criteria.

This understanding of state neutrality means government funding or accreditation/recognition (direct or indirect) is allowed regardless of the beliefs of the receiving entity, regardless of whether the beliefs are grounded in religious or secular worldviews including atheism, humanism, and other worldviews and sets of values.

SECULAR AS RELIGIOUS ABSTINENCE

The other approach to being secular is to think of it in terms of religious abstinence—secular means nonreligious. In this model, a government will not fund any program of any religious organization, nor should it directly or indirectly support a religious organization. It claims to be neutral with regard to religion in that it treats all religions equitably by not benefiting any. This is the American approach flowing out of an interpretation of their First Amendment.

In a recent case involving prayer offered at the beginning of a town council meeting and objected to by an atheist, the Supreme Court recommended abstinence—they advised that no prayer be offered. But is no prayer the neutral option? Is it not taking sides in the debate between prayer and no prayer? Some argue that this approach is fair as it treats all religions the same. However, the privatization or the banning of religion is not neutral but rather entails taking sides on how religion is expressed.

On this theme, a 1997 discussion paper of the Social Action Commission of the EFC titled "Being Christian in a Pluralistic Society" poses the following situation:

> Imagine the situation in which people are trying to agree on what sport, if any, to play. Some people want hockey, some soccer, some basketball: some want to play no sports at all. They have a definite plurality of views about sports: they discuss various compromises. Finally, someone says, "We can't play a sport that pleases everybody; it is sure to be a sport at least someone does not want. The only solution that would be fair to all is to play no sport at all." Such persons claim to be fair and impartial, but they failed see that they are offering their own preferences and rejecting everyone else's.[96]

Even the choice to do nothing is a choice.

SECULAR SECTARIANISM

The Canada Summer Jobs grant program requiring an attestation is another approach that some call secular, but that is a qualified or restricted neutrality resulting in the selective benefiting of some religious organizations. Like the fairness approach, this model technically can say it allows organizations to ground their beliefs in religion and the government does not deny a benefit because the organization is religious. However, the benefit is withheld if the organization or individual does not affirm or comply in its practices to a set of privileged values beyond the standard principles and procedures of a free and democratic government, and in the case of summer jobs, beyond what is required by employment law and health and safety regulations. By requiring adherence to an additional set of values, only those religious organizations who can ascribe to these privileged values will qualify for government funding or accreditation. These values are expressions of an ideology or worldview. They are nonreligious but are nonetheless sectarian.

The irony of the attestation is that what is required of governments, that they conform to the Charter and Charter values, is being required of organizations as a condition of receiving public funding. In a directionally plural society, our expectations of governments will be different than our expectations of other types of institutions and organizations.[97] The religion of an applicant for a government position should not be a factor, while the religion of an applicant for leadership in a religious organization is. It is the government that is expected to be nonsectarian. The purpose of the Charter is to restrict the activities of governments and government agencies and allow nongovernmental entities the freedom to manifest their distinctive culture and beliefs. By requiring compliance to the Charter, the government is imposing restrictions placed on it upon others, including nongovernmental organizations that serve specific communities.

State neutrality according to this qualified approach means that the state will not benefit or accredit any organization or individual that acts contrary to values the government champions; it is fair to all religious organizations or individuals that attest to the ideological values of the governing party. It is a sectarian approach limited to helping groups that share a commitment to certain values and rights.

We have seen that what state neutrality means varies; from the historical nonsectarian approach of religious pluralism and managing religious diversity—where the government is fair, impartial or indifferent to religious beliefs that animate those it serves and collaborates with—to an abstinence approach that seeks to detach government recognition and benefit from any religious doctrines and their institutional expression, to a sectarian approach that favours those who share the sectarian values of the government—in effect, a system of sectarian privilege. The irony is that liberalism in its inception was an attempt to avoid sectarian privilege. In Canada, however, one can find examples of all three forms of "neutrality".

TWO REGIMES OF SECULARISM

Maclure and Taylor use the language of regimes and modes of secularism to differentiate how liberal democracies attempt to balance the two major principles of secularism, equality of respect and freedom of conscience, the principles at the core of the political creed.

At the level of principles, a democratic political system recognizes the equal moral value and dignity of all citizens and therefore seeks to grant them all the same respect. Beyond these principles, the state is to be neutral towards religious and secular movements of thought. The state must not ground its decisions in any one particular religion or worldview, as the state must be able to justify to everyone decisions it makes, which it will be unable to do if it favors one particular conception of the world and of the good. Reasons justifying its actions must be "secular" or "public," that is, they must be derived from what could be called a minimal political morality potentially acceptable to all citizens.[98]

Maclure and Taylor quote Micheline Milot, who says that secularism is

a [progressive] development of the political realm by virtue of which freedom of religion and freedom of conscience are guaranteed, in conformance with a will to establish equal justice for all, by a state that is neutral towards the various conceptions of the good life coexisting in society.[99]

In terms of justifying reasons, there is considerable debate amongst liberal theorists about what would qualify as an appropriate reason, and within a directionally plural society, conceivably different reasons might be given to adherents of different comprehensive doctrines to justify the same policy.

The necessity of minimal political morality, the political creed, means that no regime will be completely nonsectarian. Maclure and Taylor make a distinction between the level of principle and the level of institutional application, that is, between moral principles such as equal respect and freedom of conscience which regulate behaviour, and concepts of neutrality, separation, and accommodation which are procedural principles that seek to institutionalize the principles of equal respect and freedom of conscience. Within secularism, there are a set of ends as well as operative modes, and these two will conflict as they cannot "coexist in perfect harmony".[100]

What Maclure and Taylor call the liberal-pluralist model is grounded in equal respect and the protection of freedom of conscience and of religion, as well as the more flexible concepts of separation of state and religion (nonsectarian, not nonreligious) and of state neutrality (fair and impartial and not abstinence). They contrast this with a more rigid form of secularism, which they call "republican", one that "allows a greater restriction on the free exercise of religion in the name of a certain understanding of the state's neutrality and of the separation of the political and religious powers."[101] So, while these "regimes of secularism" are committed to principles of equal respect and freedom of conscience, they balance these in different ways:

If respect for the equal moral value of citizens and the protection of freedom of conscience are the ends of secularism, and if the separation between the political and religious and the state's religious neutrality are means that make it possible to achieve a balance between those ends, it follows that the most rigid conceptions of secularism, quicker to set aside protections for freedom of religion, sometimes come to grant a preponderant importance to the operative modes of secularism, which are elevated to the rank of values, often at the expense of its ends. The full separation between church and state, or the state's religious neutrality, then assumes greater importance than respect for individuals' freedom of conscience.[102]

When the modes become values rather than means, or when other values are added to the two principles of equal respect and freedom of conscience and religion, the balance between equality and freedom shifts. Maclure and Taylor point out that "a regime of secularism may be more restrictive towards religious practice because it is given the mission of realizing two values besides equal respect and freedom of conscience, namely, the emancipation of individuals and civic integration."[103]

Whereas mutual respect and freedom of conscience can be understood as necessary for managing differences and living together within a directionally plural society (the requirements of minimal political morality), the emancipation of individuals and social cohesion are more aspirational. As these require a higher level of agreement on what constitutes the good life, a consensus on these will be more difficult to attain.

The promotion of the emancipation of individuals often includes promoting individual autonomy and emancipation from religion (or that which informs conscience) and could involve attempts to erode religious belief or to confine religious practice to the private sphere of familial or associative life. Either way, Maclure and Taylor contend, the principle of freedom of conscience and religion is undermined by the inclusion of conflicting principles.

> The secular state, in working towards marginalizing religion, adopts the atheists' and the agnostics' conception of the world and, consequently, does not treat with equal consideration citizens who make a place for religion in their systems of beliefs and values. That form of secularism is not neutral towards the core convictions that allow individuals to give meaning and direction to their lives. Yet the state's true commitment to individuals' moral autonomy entails the recognition that individuals are sovereign in their choices of conscience and have

the means to choose their own existential options, whether these
be secular, religious, or spiritual.[104]

The marginalizing and privatizing of religion infringe on freedom of conscience and religion and violate the very individual autonomy that the emancipation of individuals seeks to promote.

The more restrictive republican model of secularism, liberal sectarianism, also promotes the goal of civic integration: a "sense of allegiance to a common civic identity and the collective pursuit of the common good." However, they say the pursuit of civic integration need not include the effacement of difference.

While it "need not" result in the minimization of difference, it is difficult to imagine any point of integration in a society of deep directional and cultural diversity that will not marginalize some. Often the point of integration in a country is a concept of nation rooted in history, race, culture, ethnicity, and/ or language, any of which, or a combination of which, will exclude some. If the point of integration is a set of values, in the context of moral pluralism there will be dissenters who select different values or define or prioritize the selected values differently. Directional and moral differences must either be minimalized in a thin political creed, or a more robust independent ethic must be located,[105] an ethic that is claimed to be universal in its appeal to adherents of diverse comprehensive doctrines and detached from all. And, as we have seen, ultimately this imagined neutrality (and universality) is philosophically untenable. This drive for inclusion or fraternity across directional differences is an aspiration of this republican/ sectarian approach.

Hence, what emerges are two regimes or types of secularism, namely the republican model and the liberal pluralist model.

> The republican model attributes to secularism the mission of favoring, in addition to respect for moral equality and freedom of conscience, the emancipation of individuals and the growth of a common civic identity, which requires marginalizing religious affiliations and forcing them back into the private sphere. The liberal-pluralist model, by contrast, sees secularism as a mode of governance whose function is to find the optimal balance between respect for moral equality and respect for freedom of conscience. A liberal secular regime will not take exception to the mere presence of the religious in the public space and will accept the necessity of resorting to accommodations aimed at restoring equity or at allowing the exercise of freedom of religion, as long as the principle of equal respect is not

compromised. A request for accommodation would not be legitimate if it obliged the state or public institution to grant a greater value to members of a particular religion. The aim of liberal-pluralist secularism is the optimal reconciliation of the equality of respect and freedom of conscience.[106]

Regimes of secularism differ in how impartial (fair/neutral) they are towards directional pluralism. Liberal societies adopt a regime of secularism to manage directional diversity in the formation and maintenance of a political order, and the regimes will differ in how they accommodate directional pluralism depending on the form of secularism they employ. The republican version of liberalism described by Maclure and Taylor is similar to what Egerton was referring to when he used the terms "secularist" and "ideological liberal hegemony"—what I am calling liberal sectarianism. Within this republican variant of liberalism, being secular no longer means being neutral in terms of being even-handed or fair. Rather it means neutralizing the influence of religions on law and public policy and promoting sectarian values as ends—promulgating a public orthodoxy beyond the minimal political morality. In this way liberalism becomes sectarian.

The republican model adds principles to the political creed that entail a more robust idea of human flourishing that may not be commonly shared in a directionally diverse society. The state will then take sides in differences among citizens and justify its policies in one sectarian vision of life. As this is pursued, a new hegemony is advanced, and liberalism becomes secularist.

4. LIBERALISM

Liberal democracies like Canada employ a regime of secularism to regulate directional pluralism and its impact on the political order. The term *liberal* refers to a political order that seeks to provide each individual with the maximum amount of freedom to pursue their self-chosen ends, consistent with the same freedom of all others in society. A characteristic of liberalism is the formulation of a set of rights that protect individuals and minority groups from majoritarian impulses or the overreach of the state. This is the function the Charter and human rights codes are intended to serve in Canada. The limitation is the "harm principle": you are free to do what you will unless your actions harm another. The criminal code and the antidiscrimination protections offered by human rights codes are examples of restrictions placed on freedom, and they identify what our society has determined constitutes harm. They are moral codes that place limits on the exercise of freedom.

University of Toronto philosopher Ronald Beiner describes liberalism this way:

> Liberalism as I understand it does not merely refer to a particular relation between the state and the individual; rather it expresses an encompassing view of human life, one that aspires to leave individuals as much as possible to shape their lives according to their own notions, so that the society offers no official guidance on how people are to conduct their lives in a meaningful direction.[107]

Liberalism embraces a form of secularism to politically manage directional diversity within a specific political jurisdiction (a state). The selection of the regime of secularism chosen by democratic governments and those who elect them—say, between the liberal pluralist mode and the republican/sectarian mode as described by Maclure and Taylor—will depend on the relative balance desired between equal respect, freedom of conscience, the emancipation of individuals, and civic integration.

Historically, in the aftermath of the Reformation, when different traditions of Christianity competed for the allegiance of people, there were conflicts between various Christian traditions at a time when each state was intertwined with one specific Christian tradition (for example, the king or queen of England being the head of the Anglican church and defender of the faith).

Bruce J. Clemenger

With dissenting Christian minorities (the nonconformists) facing discrimination and persecution, liberalism emerged as a way of understanding how the state could perform its functions without any formal ties to, or the promotion of, any one Christian tradition. Liberalism tried to imagine a way of statecraft and the process of identifying and applying governing political principles and procedures without reliance upon, or direct connection to, any particular Christian tradition (the separation of state and church). At a time when the divine right of the monarch was commonly held and freedoms were being wrested away at the whims of monarchs, it was difficult to envision how statecraft could be expressed apart from a distinctive Catholic, or Anglican, or even Reformed theology (think of Calvin's Geneva). Inculcating the principles of equal respect and freedom of conscience was critical to fostering tolerance in a directionally diverse society.

TOLERATION, THE SOCIAL CONTRACT, AND VIEWS OF HUMAN NATURE

John Locke's famous "Letter Concerning Toleration", published in 1689, was one response to the challenge of Christian pluralism. Locke advocated the toleration of various religions. However, he limited toleration to some Christian traditions but not to all; Catholics were not to be tolerated, as, he argued, they owed their allegiance to a foreign prince (the pope). Neither were atheists to be tolerated, as those who did not believe in God could not be trusted. From his exceptions and the rationale he offered, you can see the issues with which he and his peers were grappling. In the case of Canada and its founding constitution, it was necessary to locate a basis for the political order that was not reliant on theological doctrines that would divide Protestants and Roman Catholics and would therefore promote tolerance.

In attempting to propose an alternative basis, Locke envisioned a state of nature without any system of government in which the people would form a social contract one with another, the contract establishing a set of principles which would guide their lives together in the public sphere. This social contract would become the basis for government and would not be rooted in any one specific Christian tradition or set of doctrines.

Of course, the depiction of the state of nature would entail some assumptions about human nature and the purpose of human life. Subsequent depictions of the state of nature proposed by various philosophers would entail different assumptions and, as a result, different understandings of the principles of the social contract. Locke's state of nature was premised on an idyllic view of the Americas (indigenous people living in relative harmony), whereas the state of nature described by Hobbes was framed by a dim view of human nature and of life, which he described as "solitary, poor, nasty, brutish, and short". As a result, Locke's social contract focuses on principles of cooperation and increased influence of elected representatives, whereas Hobbes's political order is authoritarian. To be legitimate, the political order would need to be seen to respect the principles of the social contract.[108]

OVERLAPPING CONSENSUS LIBERALISM

The most influential delineation of contemporary liberalism based on a social contract theory was provided by Harvard's John Rawls in his books *A Theory of Justice* (1971) and *Political Liberalism* (1996).

Rather than positing a state of nature as Locke or Hobbes did, Rawls envisions what he calls an original position in which people are unaware of their identities, including their religious beliefs, their sex, ethnicity, race, and economic or social status. They're behind what he calls a "veil of ignorance". His contention is that reasonable people behind a veil of ignorance will agree to some basic principles of justice, being careful not to build in any bias towards any characteristic they might or, more importantly, might not have.

These principles of justice are rooted neither in anyone's comprehensive doctrine nor in any specific vision of the good, as people behind the veil do not know what belief system they affirm. He says the resulting principles of justice are the conclusions of reasonable people. He argues that these principles of justice will be acceptable to anyone who would adhere to a reasonable comprehensive doctrine because the principles of justice will enable them to pursue their own vision of the good life. (This is tautological—reasonable person would not subscribe to an unreasonable comprehensive doctrine.) Rawls refers to this agreement on principles as an overlapping consensus.

The conditions of the veil of ignorance are hypothetical. The idea is grounded in a presumption that the human person can deliberate apart from any attachments or characteristics (the premise of individual autonomy), that reason is not conditioned by different worldviews but universal, and that this unencumbered self provides a truly unbiased vantage point from which to identify a notion of justice apart from any reference to a conception of the good. Individual autonomy is presumed. While it might be imagined in a hypothetical social contract negotiation, it can also become a presumption about the human condition: the belief that only as autonomous beings are we free, and any harm or disadvantage resulting from the personal characteristics we have (sex, race, religion, economic or social status) will be mitigated by the principles we design.

Bruce J. Clemenger

As noted earlier and as Maclure and Taylor have reminded us, the consensus upon which a liberal political regime is grounded is not ultimately neutral. Liberalism will champion specific principles (a minimal political morality or a political creed) which will be more directly aligned with some comprehensive doctrines than with others. For example, a stress on individual freedom may not mesh well with a system of belief and practice that promotes the communal over the individual (the premise of individual autonomy agitates against a communal premise of human life). The political regime will be successful and find legitimacy in the eyes of its citizens if the political principles of the consensus are understood to be authentic expressions of, or principles that are consistent with, each of the doctrines adhered to by the citizens; that is, if it is the result of a convergence on common or shared principles that all can affirm.

Maclure and Taylor say a state that embraces these common political principles cannot itself adopt any one of the "core or meaning-giving beliefs and commitments"—which are multiple and sometimes difficult to reconcile—that citizens espouse. By the terms,

> core or meaning-giving beliefs and commitments we understand the reasons, evaluations, or grounds stemming from the conception of the world or of the good adopted by individuals that allow them to understand the world around them and to give meaning and direction to their lives. It is in choosing values, hierarchizing or reconciling them, and clarifying the projects based on them that human beings manage to structure their existence, to exercise their judgment, and to conduct their life—in short, to constitute a moral identity for themselves.[109]

Human dignity would be an example of a doctrine that most would affirm and which serves as the basis for principles of freedom and equality.

Maclure and Taylor describe this convergence:

> The crux of the matter is that citizens come together on the basis of their own perspective, around a common set of principles that can ensure social cooperation and political stability. Peaceful coexistence will be based not on the secular equivalent of a religious doctrine but, rather, on a range of values and principles that can be the object of an overlapping consensus. The aim of relying on common public values is to ensure the moral equality of citizens so that, potentially, they

can all embrace the state's broad orientations on the basis of their own conception of the good.[110]

The task of liberalism is to identify the rules of our living together—the social contract—without direct reliance on any specific comprehensive doctrine. Maclure and Taylor would contend that two principles that meet this test are equal respect and freedom of conscience.

CONVERGENCE OR CONSENSUS LIBERALISM

Note that while Jocelyn Maclure and Charles Taylor use John Rawls's language of overlapping consensus, they do not affirm the view of many liberals, including Rawls, that the principles of the consensus are freestanding—that is, that they are formed or held independent of the religious or secular doctrines citizens hold. (The original position of Rawls proposes to identify principles of justice apart from an appeal to comprehensive doctrines.)

To understand this distinction, I return to John Gray's depiction of convergence liberalism mentioned earlier, which he distinguishes from consensus liberalism. In one approach, the principles and values of the social contract would be consistent with the convergence of agreement on what civility and justice mean, drawn from the various traditions and systems of beliefs and thus the various understandings of the good that are adhered to by Canadians. This convergence is a modus vivendi forged in a dialogue of the doctrines finding adherents in a society. Common principles and shared social norms will guide the political order which is not sectarian (is secular) and is impartial (is neutral) towards the comprehensive doctrines to which citizens, equal members in the social contract, adhere. Gray calls this the convergence type of liberalism.

Gray says the alternative face of liberalism is the fermentation of a consensus on a set of principles that over time become detached from the originating and sustaining doctrines, gain primacy in the public realm, and become the requirement of good citizenship. These trump all other allegiances in the public sphere and become what Taylor has described as an independent ethic. Under this type of consensus, there is pressure for dissenting religions and sets of doctrines to be relegated to the private realm or to be more conducive to the public ethos, while the public realm is governed by the consensus to which all are expected to adhere as citizens. The consensus is no longer understood to be an overlapping consensus of the various religious traditions adhered to but is detached, viewed as freestanding, and expressed independently from these moorings as it claims supremacy in public and shared spaces. It becomes something to which all are expected to adhere in the political and public sphere.

Becoming detached, it takes on a life of its own; it is presented as reasonable and neutral, and something to which all citizens should adhere publicly. It is no longer seen as a product of convergence but as an agreement that must prevail if it comes into conflict with the comprehensive doctrines that contributed to its formation. This is why it is incumbent on the adherents of the various comprehensive doctrines to understand their respective reasons and rationales for forging the contract and to engage when the contract is interpreted in a way that conflicts with the contributing doctrines. John Rawls wanted to identify a contract that is more stable than a convergence or modus vivendi and not vulnerable to renegotiation; hence his desire to establish a contract that would find adherence from reasonable people regardless of their comprehensive doctrines.

Maclure and Taylor warn that this form of secularism

> takes pride in its neutrality toward the different religions but does not adopt a true position of neutrality at the level of the conception of the good. On the contrary, in its most radical form it appeals to an "independent morality" founded on the principles of reason and on a particular conception of human nature.[111]

In other words, if a particular understanding of human nature and reasoning is embraced, then the resulting morality presents as something that all reasonable persons can or should embrace. This political ideology replaces established religion with a secularist moral philosophy. Borrowing the expression of Jean-Jacques Rousseau, Maclure and Taylor say that such a moral and political philosophy is a civil religion.

Take, for example, the principle of human dignity. All major religions as well as humanists and others affirm some variant of the dignity of the human person. There is a convergence on this principle. We can each affirm it from out of our respective faith or religious or ideological traditions. However, what happens when the interpretation and application of human dignity no longer reflects the convergence and its interpretation and application clash, for example, with the principle of freedom of expression or of conscience? My desire for medical assistance in dying (euthanasia), which it is now understood as an extension of my dignity, conflicts with your freedom of conscience as a doctor to not participate in assisting me to die. In a convergence scenario, an interpretation of human dignity that conflicts with the religious/philosophical traditions that comprise the convergence cannot be imposed. Accommodation must be offered to those refusing to participate. Or the act is decriminalized and not legalized which removes an obligation to fund it. It is permissible, but no one is compelled to assist. In other words, the doctor keeps his or her job and the patient finds another doctor.

In a consensus scenario, the sectarian interpretation of dignity might be embedded in legislation legalizing the practice and be imposed on the consciences of those opposed. A current example is the requirement of the College of Physicians and Surgeons of Ontario that doctors must facilitate at minimum an effective referral for procedures such as assisted suicide or abortion, in case a doctor might object to participating for reasons of conscience or religious beliefs. While other jurisdictions have found ways to accommodate dissenting doctors, Ontario is insisting that doctors must provide all legal and funded services.

Certainly, a common or shared vision of the public good is necessary to evoke allegiance to a set of societal norms that enables a society to function well. Either the common principles are the result of a convergence of the respective doctrines of the various significant spiritual forces adhered to within society, or a consensus needs to be forged and sustained that can operate independently of directional plurality.

If the consensus is established and enforced through law (the stick) and by granting government benefits (the carrot), then when the consensus—or more specifically, when the interpretation of the principles of the consensus—conflicts with the principles of a given religious tradition, the consensus is expected to trump the tradition: citizens are pressured socially and economically to affirm the consensus despite their religious convictions. Such an affirmation concedes that religion can be relegated to the private sphere and that something else governs the public sphere.

As I wrote in a *Faith Today* column,

> Our faith instructs us that, if Jesus is not Lord of an area of our life, then something or someone else is. Our western culture tells us there are areas of life that are "a-religious" or religiously neutral, that we can separate facts from values and faith from reason, and that when we step out of our churches and enter the public square, we need to ensure our religious identity does not infringe on our ability to adopt a secular stance and behave as secularists want us to behave—like them.[112]

The type of liberalism that shaped the Canadian political order these past decades was a convergence form of liberalism that reflected Christian pluralism as described by Egerton. Laws enacted and policies implemented could not stray too far from the public morality deeply influenced by Christianity and embraced by most Canadians. The shift to a secularist pluralism meant law, and the political order more generally, needed to find an alternative, secular grounding. The Charter can be understood and interpreted as either a convergence document, where its interpretation must be in alignment with the various directional affirmations of Canadians, or as a consensus document whose interpretation is based on principles derived from other sources.

In a 2005 speech, Chief Justice McLachlin of the Supreme Court stated:

> The contemporary concept of unwritten constitutional principles can be seen as a modern reincarnation of the ancient doctrines of natural law. Like those conceptions of justice, the identification of these principles seems to presuppose the existence of some kind of natural order. Unlike them, however, it does not fasten upon theology as the source of the unwritten principles that transcend the exercise of state power. It is derived from the history, values and culture of the nation, viewed in its historical context.[113]

The "history, values and culture" of Canada were deeply shaped by Christianity, but the influence of religion is in danger of being erased in the understanding of our history. As noted above, John Webster Grant forewarned that Canada's history could be told without reference to religion. A current example is the book *The Canadian Manifesto*, in which Conrad Black tells the history of Canada and identifies strategies and policies that will fulfill Canada's promise going forward.[114] There is, however, scant reference to the shaping influence of Christianity or of churches, nor is there any mention of the role of religion or religious institutions in the future development of Canada.

While Christianity and liberalism both shaped the political order in Canada, will the liberal side of the equation become the sole interpretive framework for the development of law and the application of the Charter going forward? It is important to remember that the rights guaranteed in several sections of the Charter can be circumscribed if doing so is justifiable in a free and democratic society. The meaning of "free and democratic" becomes determinative, and whoever defines the meaning of this phrase shapes the application of the Charter. Will ideas of natural law and of a natural order still be entertained as part of the sources of the convergence? More generally, will the Charter be interpreted as a product of convergence and be interpreted in the light of the various comprehensive doctrines to which Canadians adhere, including religious ones? Or will it be promulgated as an articulation of a consensus understood in secularist terms which defines and regulates Canadian public life?

Recall that Maclure and Taylor noted it is the additional principles of individual emancipation and civic integration that can tilt liberalism from a pluralist to a republican (sectarian) expression. If the state adopts the emancipation of individuals as a purpose, then it will work to promote individual autonomy and the disestablishment of that which hinders the free choice of individuals. If conscience is an expression of norms and beliefs held by a person, then emancipation entails ensuring the person can challenge and test those norms and beliefs. Freedom to choose trumps freedom to adhere. If civic integration becomes a purpose of the state, then it will seek to promote integration that supersedes, at least in the political sphere, any other attachment.

THE EMERGING NATURE OF LIBERALISM

Is this movement to a republican or public sectarian variant inevitable? Maclure and Taylor present it as a choice. Others, like George Grant, Eric Voegelin, and, more recently, Patrick Deneen, see a shift to a more ideological liberalism as something inherent in the logic of liberalism, though they do so for different (through interrelated) reasons.

Canadian philosopher George Grant detects in liberalism a trajectory which inevitably drives to the embrace of a progressive liberalism rooted in individual autonomy, a view of the human person that conflicts with that of many comprehensive doctrines including those rooted in the Christian tradition. While the commitment to human autonomy has become widespread and was not seen as problematic when Grant warned of its acceptance in the early 1960s, it is worthwhile to recall his deep reservations about the concept and its general acceptance.

Grant defines liberalism as "a set of beliefs which proceed from the central assumption that man's essence is his freedom and therefore that which chiefly concerns man in this life is to shape the world as we want it."[115] Calling it "English-speaking liberalism," he says it is a certain species of liberalism that, for Canadians, is our moral tradition rooted in a "belief that political liberty is a central human good."[116] He says that the social contract of this liberalism centers around the protection of the rights of individuals. As utilitarianism—centered on the idea of the greatest good for the greatest number—can fail to protect minorities or those with little influence, liberalism contends that free and rational individuals will seek a political order that protects the rights of all individuals:

> The good society is composed of free individuals who agree
> to live together only on the condition that the rules of
> cooperation, necessary to that living together, serve the overall

> purposes of each member of that society. That agreement or contract, and the calculating implicit in it, is the only model of political relations adequate to autonomous adults. The state must be such that each person can freely agree to limitations it imposes, and this will only be possible when its free, rational members know that its existence is, in the main, to their advantage.[117]

As Grant summarizes liberalism, rather than grounding political order in an understanding that humans are directed to a certain highest good or a specific idea of justice, the idea is that the state would be agnostic about the highest good and, rather, function as if grounded in a social contract between free calculating individuals, their freedom limited only at activity that infringes on the external freedom of others. Justice becomes contractual, and the argument is that the state does not impose moral duties; it simply enforces the social contract. Religion and morality are private matters, and society "is organized for the pursuit of individual interests in general".[118]

While this may seem to be fair, it is incompatible with those who reject its individualist premise or those who are vulnerable to being left out of the contract. The argument is that establishing the contract does not require agreement on what is good. The state based on the contract is believed to be morally neutral because "the principles of justice can be clearly determined quite outside any opinions concerning that possibility".[119] This is the fallacy of the social contract (as noted above). It is not detached or freestanding but is forged out of convergence of people agreeing to the principles of the contract based on the comprehensive doctrines to which they adhere. It is not morally neutral.

Like Maclure and Taylor, Grant was concerned with the privatizing of directional pluralism. Maclure and Taylor argue for a regime of secularism that would provide for the public expression of directional diversity, and Grant warns of the implications of privatization. He says that within liberalism,

> Philosophy or religion becomes comparable to the question of sexual habits. They are simply a matter of private pursuit, unless their conclusions interfere with the liberty of others ... Philosophy and religion can be allowed to be perfectly free because their conclusions are perfectly private.[120]

In the pursuit of freedom for autonomous individuals, the state, he says, must pursue equality in all aspects of life, including civil liberties and the provision of self-respect.

Rejecting liberalism's claims of neutrality, that it has no specific notion of the highest good and that it does not impose moral duties, Grant says liberalism is a political morality which entails assumptions about human and nonhuman nature. Rather than a convergence on a set of principles and procedures to order our lives together within the context of directional pluralism, he says liberalism is an ideology: a surrogate religion masquerading as philosophy.[121]

The liberalism that Grant describes requires a moral philosophy. He contends that secular liberalism depended on Protestantism in English-speaking societies for its "moral bite".[122] To illustrate this need, he asks why should anyone sacrifice for the common good if avoidance of violent death is our highest end?[123] A convergence liberalism would not demand such sacrifice, but its constitutive comprehensive doctrines might. How then does the consensus liberalism organized around individual autonomy come to where it can demand sacrifice unless it functions as a surrogate religion? In the case of "English Speaking Justice," Grant says it was Protestantism that provided the moral cement, as justice is more than a convenient contract.

He says initially Protestantism accepted the contract for practical reasons: recall Egerton's depiction of the mutual support between Christianity and liberalism in the Christian pluralism phase in Canada. However, Grant says:

> The more Protestants came to be influenced by the theoretical foundations of the liberalism they had first accepted for practical reasons, the less were they able to sustain their prime theological belief which had allowed them to support justice in a more than contractual way; therefore, they were less able to provide the moral cement which had given vigor to the liberal regime. The more secular liberals were able to make it explicit that their belief in freedom was not simply a matter of political consent, but implied that human beings were makers of their own laws, the less could they receive from their Protestant supporters that moral force which made their regimes nobler than an individualism which calculated its contracts.[124]

He says, "the secularizing of the Protestant faith was impacted on the scientific side by the work of Darwin, and on the philosophical side the work of the Enlightenment."[125] On the philosophic side, as "enlightened" human beings came to express their self-understanding as autonomy—that is, to believe themselves the makers of their own laws—any formulation of Christianity became unthinkable.[126]

Protestantism had set the parameters of decency and those who acted "outside of these parameters had rightly to feel or assume shame".[127] With the weakening of the beliefs and institutions that sustained civil society, specifically Protestantism, what is filling the void? What institutions will replace the churches and Christianity, and will guide our morality? What will regulate our choices and how we treat one another? Using John Webster Grant's language, who now would mold the character of Canadians and sustain the moral and spiritual foundations of nationhood? Grant says Protestantism lost its ability to provide a public sense of justice beyond the contractual account as it absorbed the liberalism rooted in the idea of autonomous will. In its development liberalism was

> enfolded in a sufficiently widespread public religion to produce believers who accepted the liberal state, and yet did not believe that justice was good simply because it was the product of calculated contract. The story has been told many times of how most intellectuals in our societies scorned the fundamental beliefs of the public religion, and yet counted on the continuance of its moral affirmations to serve as a convenient public basis of justice.[128]

However, Grant says that liberalism could not quickly kill the presence of eternity given in the day-to-day life of justice.[129] He expressed concern over whether justice can be sustained in a world if it is considered simply a chosen convenience. A mere social contract cannot answer the key question liberalism must answer: "What is it, if anything, about human beings that makes the rights of equal justice their due?" He continues, "The need to justify modern liberal justice has been kept in the wings of our English-speaking drama by our power and the strength of our tradition."[130]

According to Grant's account, liberalism is a form of secularized Christianity which permeates Canadian society. Grant says, "Justice as equality and fairness is that bit of Christian instinct that survives the death of God."[131] It is Christianity that insists on the primacy of charity and its implications for equality. He says that for Christians, "the substance of our belief is that the perfect living out of that justice is unfolded in the Gospels."[132] The message is that "justice is what we are fitted for." Can a secular ideology provide a similar ethos?

Another challenge noted by Maclure and Taylor and discussed by Grant is the conflict between liberty and equality in the provision of primary goods. Liberalism must determine which goods are necessary to liberty and equality, and this will necessitate the construction of a public ideology to answer these questions and legitimize the conclusions, as well as support the laws and policies that advance them. Grant warns that under these conditions, autonomy directing justice, the pursuit of the equality of primary goods "will exclude liberal justice from those who are too weak to enforce contracts—the imprisoned, the mentally unstable, the unborn, the aged, the defeated and sometimes even the morally un-conforming."[133]

As the state is to promote autonomy and equality, it must identify the requisite primary goods, that is, the key means which free individuals must have to pursue their self-interest and preserve their autonomy and equality. These goods, which he calls cozy pleasures, must be maximized. The drive for what Maclure and Taylor called individual emancipation may take precedence over securing other primary "goods". The identification of specific primary goods entails a type of conception of the common good to which society must be ordered. This moves beyond the contractual nature of Gray's convergence type of liberalism and of Maclure and Taylor's liberal-pluralist secularism. It is characteristic of the ideological liberal hegemony identified by Egerton.

Grant and others have pointed out that some anthropology will underlie any depiction of a state of nature. Grant says that in accepting liberalism, Protestants "were giving up the doctrine of creation as the primal teaching".[134] Rather, they would choose principles to order their activity in the public sphere that are acceptable to all rational human beings. In effect, liberalism is premised on the idea that the human species "depends for its progress not on God or nature but on its own freedom, and the direction of that progress is determined by the fact that we can rationally give ourselves our own moral laws."[135]

As noted above, a political system that replaces established religion with a secularist moral philosophy is a secular "civil religion". It plays the role Christianity once had in Canada. In the republican variant of liberalism, the state intentionally reinforces and promotes the liberal moral philosophy in the broader society, through the public education system, for example. In Gray's terms, it is a consensus type of liberalism that has fostered an independent morality rooted in an anthropology framed by individual autonomy. It has replaced Christianity in Canada as the public religion while seeking to sustain some aspects of Christianity to secure some moral supports. While it may aspire to being neutral and nonsectarian, its underlying commitments will privilege comprehensive doctrines that are similarly liberal or which champion the primary goods consistent with liberalism. Related to this theme is the problem also found in Rawls's theory, namely, the nonneutrality of a technological society and the shaping influence it has often expressed in the impulse that "what technological can do, it must". In its ideological form it challenges the religious and cultural ways of life of some communities such as the Amish. Not all devices are "neutral" when it comes to life-transforming trajectories (for good or ill).

Within liberalism,

> the language of traditional religion can sustain itself in the public realm only insofar as it responds to the issues on the same side as the dominating liberalism. If it does, it is allowed to express itself about social issues. But if there is a conflict between the religious voices and liberalism, then the religious voices are condemned as reactionary and told to confine themselves to the proper place of religion, which is the private realm.[136]

The public expression of religion is welcome if it is liberal and does not challenge the public religion.

Similar to George Grant's depiction of the trajectory of liberalism, other scholars have also concluded that the inner dynamic of liberalism causes it not to be static but unfolding and that the evolution of a liberal sectarianism is an outworking of the very nature of liberalism. Catholic historian Christopher Dawson describes liberalism as a midpoint in the unfolding of the logic of secularism. "Once society is launched on the path of secularization it cannot stop in the half-way house of liberalism; it must go on to the bitter end, whether that end be Communism or some alternative type of totalitarian secularism."[137]

In a similar fashion, philosopher Eric Voegelin describes the trajectory of liberalism as having a revolutionary impulse that is expressed in four areas; the political, economic, religious, and scientific.[138]

Politically, it is defined by its claims to oppose certain abuses and any order based on privileged position. Voegelin says the problem is that while this attack was originally led by the liberal bourgeoisie, the attack on privilege turns on the bourgeoisie, and the revolutionary movement cannot end until society has become egalitarian. Economically, liberalism seeks to repeal legal restrictions that set limits on economic activity and believes there should be no principle or no motive of economic activity other than enlightened self-interest. All barriers (including national ones) to trade and economic progress should be eradicated. Religiously, liberalism rejects revelation and dogma as sources of truth; it discards spiritual substance and becomes secularistic and ideological. Last, scientifically it assumes that autonomous, immanent human reason is the source of all knowledge. Science is free research liberated from authorities, not only from revelation and dogmatism but from classical philosophy as well.[139]

As a revolutionary movement, liberalism continues to press for reform and, according to Voegelin, will not result in a stable condition until its goal is achieved. It continues to press towards an "eschatological final state" characterized by true freedom and equality. Voegelin says,

> One can't get away from the revolution. Whoever participates in it for a time with the intention of retiring peacefully with a pension which calls itself liberalism will discover sooner or later that the revolutionary convulsion to destroy socially harmful, obsolete institutions is not a good investment for a pensioner.[140]

I recall attending a lunchtime session hosted at Osgoode Hall Law School which was, in effect, the celebration of the recent court decision to extend marriage to same-sex couples in 2003. It was a most telling experience. One of the participants was the first homosexual man to be married in the province of Ontario, and he said that he and his new spouse merely wanted to be treated as any other married couple. They wanted to live on a quiet street with their dog amongst other married couples.

A woman objected to this dream. She described herself as a feminist and was deeply troubled with the picture he painted. In her mind, marriage itself represented a harmful patriarchy, and her intent as a lesbian feminist was to gain access to marriage to deconstruct it from within. So, while the recently married gay man had achieved his goal, she wanted to continue the process which would, in the end, deconstruct that which he fought to attain. Once he attained his goal, he wanted the revolution to stop. She wanted it to continue and believed the logic of the revolution would eventually deconstruct that which he fought to attain. These tensions belie the expectation that individual human autonomy can be a sufficient basis for a stable society in which all can flourish.

Voegelin sees liberalism as a phase of a broader political movement, something which always moves. The phases of the political movement are revolution, restoration, conservatism, and liberalism, the latter three being modes of reaction to revolution. For example, conservatives are often influenced by liberal ideas of a generation ago; they are "old style" liberals. Voegelin writes, "In the American political vocabulary liberal generally means, not the European liberalism of the nineteenth century, which today is considered conservative, but on the contrary a politically progressive attitude."[141]

Following Charles Comte's notion of a permanent revolution ever progressing to an ideal state, liberalism continually presses and becomes a politics of reform that thwarts revolutionary terror. The goal is peaceful change, and "liberalism becomes a method for carrying on the revolution with other, less destructive means." As a movement, its goal is not a stable condition, but a constant press for change. Voegelin says to continually strive for progress towards a final state of rational humanity and a more perfect community of freedom, equality, and fraternity, to reach a state of everlasting peace will, in the end, require a transformation of human nature. "The unchangeable nature of man constantly places obstacles in the path to the paradisiacal goal. If the goal of the revolution is defined by a gnostic philosophy of history, then revolutionary action has no rational goal."[142]

The final goal of liberalism cannot be attained, he concludes. Philosophically liberalism breaks down beliefs but has nothing to put in their place. Rather liberalism is a phase, politically pressing for egalitarianism and against privilege, the separation of powers and any tie between state and church. Economically, it is against limits to free activity, and religiously it challenges revelation and dogma as sources of truth. Scientifically its essence is "the assumption of the autonomy of immanent reason as the source of knowledge".[143] As liberalism progresses, it will require, as George Grant argues, an alternative spiritual order to replace Christianity, which provided the context within which the tenets of liberalism originated. Progressive liberalism will be incompatible with some comprehensive doctrines and hence incompatible with the liberal-pluralist model. This new liberalism lacks tolerance towards any opposing worldview, including the variant of the liberalism it sought to sustain within a Christianity it now rejects.[144]

Patrick Deneen in his book *Why Liberalism Failed* also reflects on this trajectory of liberalism. He says liberalism has failed because it has been "true to itself". Inner logic has become more evident and its self-contradictions manifest:

> A political philosophy that was launched to foster greater equity, defend a pluralist tapestry of different cultures and beliefs, protect human dignity, and, of course, expand liberty, in practice generates titanic inequality, enforces uniformity and homogeneity, fosters material and spiritual degradation, and undermines freedom … As an ideology, [liberalism] pretends to neutrality, claiming no preference and denying any intention of shaping souls under its rule. It ingratiates by invitation.[145]

In this form, liberalism is more than a commitment to certain principles: it is an ideology or moral philosophy and is a replacement religion to the one it seeks to transform. Following James Skillen, if we define religion as human convictions, presuppositions, and commitments that give fundamental direction to human actions and moral arguments, this form of liberalism will qualify. Skillen writes, "The deepest presuppositions of so-called secular philosophies function in the same way as do the deepest presuppositions of traditional religions."[146] The Enlightenment and Communism, he says, "by this interpretation are as religiously profound and comprehensive as any outlook fostered by a historical religion … No argument about bad law or good law can proceed without reference to normative ideas of authority and freedom, of human dignity and responsibility." By this analysis, this type of liberalism, as all political/legal systems around the world, has its historical origins in a particular "religious" vision of life. Even so-called secular approaches to political life, says Skillen, are themselves thoroughly religious in nature.[147]

As we have seen the guiding spirit of liberalism is the pursuit of freedom and equality, and it entails a specific understanding of human nature, of normativity, and of knowledge. As an ideology it shapes people's perceptions of themselves and societal institutions, conforming both to its understanding of truth. It will require deference in the public sphere.

FREEDOM AND EQUALITY

The moral claim of liberalism, emanating from its sectarian stance, is disclosed in the definitions it gives to the core principles of freedom and equality. As discussed in Part One, and as described by Dickerson and Flanagan, key liberal principles have changed in meaning over time. Does freedom mean the absence of coercion or the ability to pursue chosen ends? Politically, the former would require a minimalist state (which leaves the individual alone unless the individual violates the same right of others to be left alone), while the latter would expect a more engaged state that is concerned with not only the absence of coercion but the presence of means or capacity necessary for the expression of freedom (individual emancipation).

John Gray says the understanding of freedom as autonomy can be dated back to John Stuart Mill's *On Liberty*. Gray says,

> Freedom no longer refers only, or even mainly, to protection from coercion by the law or other people—a system of toleration—but to a radical type of personal autonomy—the ability to create an identity and a style of life for oneself without regard for public opinion or any external authority. In future, only a single type of life would be tolerated—one based on individual choice.[148]

Does equality mean all are treated the same (justice is blind) or that not only one's dignity be respected but that one's choices be affirmed? The shift from equal respect as the legal equality of personhood to equal respect for choices likewise requires a more interventionist state through the development of policies that address inequities as well as initiatives that silence any judgment for the choices people make. Thus, the primary role of government will range from enforcing basic rules and preventing people from harming each other through force or fraud (a "night watchman" state), to promoting freedom in the sense of capacity, offering promises of social welfare and reducing differences in order to ensure that no one is prevented by others from having a chance to achieve success, and promoting the celebration of choices people make (diversity, inclusion, and equity, for example).

The dilemma for liberalism here, as noted by Maclure and Taylor as well as Grant, is that the pursuits of freedom and equality are often in conflict, and the meanings given each will impact how directional pluralism is managed. Taylor writes:

> The liberal state, for example, defends the principle that individuals are to be considered autonomous moral agents, free to the find their own conception of the good life. In the schools, therefore, the state will favor the development of students' critical autonomy. In exposing students to plurality of worldviews and modes of life, the democratic and liberal state makes the task more difficult for parents seeking to transmit a particular order of beliefs to their children and even more difficult for groups wishing to shield themselves from the influence of the larger society in order to perpetuate a style of life based more on respect for tradition than on individual autonomy and the exercise of critical judgment.[149]

The meaning given the terms will affect the interpretation and application of the political creed and the scope of state action. This conflict, both between the definitions of freedom and equality respectively, or between the two principles themselves, is expressed through the formation of political parties that differ in their interpretation of these principles and the relative priority they assign to each.

Certainly, Christians affirm freedom and equality, and we recognize the value of democratic processes and of limits on government power. As George Grant maintains, freedom and equality are Christian principles. However, as Maclure and Taylor and others have warned, liberalism is not neutral with respect to a plurality of comprehensive doctrines, the application of the principles, and the institutional expression given to these. Different forms or regimes of liberalism will define core terms differently and influence how they manage and accommodate directional diversity. Various forms will be more amenable to some comprehensive doctrines than to others, as exemplified in the difference between the liberal-pluralist and the republican (liberal sectarianism) forms of liberalism and the mode of secularism each employs.

INDIVIDUAL AUTONOMY

Increasingly in Canada, the prime commitment of liberalism is to individual autonomy understood as individual emancipation and self-determination. At a 2020 forum on end of life, equality, and disability, the Canadian justice minister said the task of governments "is allowing people to flourish and live in a way they want to live, choose to live, and in order to make autonomy a real and robust concept".[150] At the same event another federal minster said, "Personal autonomy is a sacred right, a sacred choice to be able to make the choices for yourself, about yourself, and the life you choose to live." If autonomy is a sacred right and the task of government is to make autonomy a real and robust concept, then it becomes a goal of the liberal state to remove any barriers that hinder individual autonomy.

Autonomy is atomistic in that it understands the individual to be the locus of authority and meaning.[151] J.M. Keynes warned of the implications of individualism, saying:

> The world is not so governed from above that private and social interests always coincide. It is not so managed here below that in practice they coincide. It is not a correct deduction from the principles of economics that enlightened self-interest always operates in the public interest. Nor is it true that self-interest generally is enlightened: more often individuals acting separately to promote their own ends are too ignorant or too weak to attain these.[152]

According to individual autonomy, only individuals have ontic or moral status. Associations are nothing more than an aggregate of self-determining individuals who cooperate because they share a common interest or purpose. All social institutions have only a derived, and therefore tentative, contractual existence. Their authority and power over the individual are carefully delimited. Forms such as the family and the state are deemed necessary but are considered human-made and artificial entities and are considered potential threats to the autonomy of the individual.

Thus, the family is merely an interacting framework for developing the rights and abilities of each family member, marriage is merely a contract which is binding if the participants agree, a business is an artificial entity in which economic transactions take place among freely competing individuals, and a church is something akin to a cultural association and formed for the private benefit of its members. Society is seen as an aggregate of self-determining individuals tending toward a state of natural autonomy and the state is an instrument through which rational self-determining individuals can be assured of having their basic liberties protected and their pursuit of autonomy enabled. The political order exists solely to safeguard the purposes of autonomous individuals. This atomistic view of the individual is incompatible with more holistic understandings of personhood and clashes with more communitarian understandings such as those of Indigenous peoples.

In reflecting on the sanctity of human life court cases we were intervening on, I wrote:

> In its philosophical sense, autonomy presumes no prior and external authority to the self ... all attachments that once were understood to comprise personhood are secondary and artificial—our identity is something we create by an exercise of our will. There is normativity. Legitimacy is [now] something we confer, not acknowledge ... what was once held to be illegal to protect us all now becomes legal for the sake of a few.[153]

Justice is understood to be rooted in intuitive ideas that all rational individuals will affirm and can be identified apart from any appeal to the good, or so the proponents contend. The rational person, in establishing what justice is, can distance themselves from their religious and cultural context and function as an "unencumbered self" who is autonomous (able to choose ends) and is an individual (identifiable apart from their religious, ethnic, familial, and cultural rootedness—living behind Rawls's veil of ignorance).[154] Within this individualist framing, these choices can become disembodied. At our core we are self-interested calculators, and we are separable from these other attachments. It is on this core self that autonomy-promoting liberalism is premised.

5. A POST-LIBERAL SECTARIANISM: IS PLURALIST LIBERALISM STILL A VIABLE OPTION?

Liberal advocates' appeal to all is that they seek to maximize each person's freedom to pursue a life they each think is worth living and thereby provide the best political order for accommodating directional diversity. Given the spectre of a sectarian liberalism, is a liberal pluralist nonsectarian solution still possible?

Taylor and Maclure believe the commitment to equality of respect and freedom of conscience are the necessary commitments to an open pluralism that will provide substantial freedom and accommodation for directional pluralism. They contend that these two principles would be affirmed by those who adhere to a variety of visions of the good and will provide a public space within which diverse worldviews can be expressed and can form the basis of collaboration across directional differences, including in the political sphere. It is not impartial, though its political creed is minimal.

They contrast their approach with a republican liberalism which adds individual emancipation and social cohesion to the basic principles of the state. They warn that the addition of these will influence the balance in safeguarding equal respect and freedom of conscience.

Cécile Laborde locates republicanism between the tradition of egalitarian liberalism represented by John Rawls and Maclure and Taylor, and communitarianism. Republicanism is distinctive in its primary emphasis on citizenship and the civic virtues which all citizens are expected to share and affirm. As Laborde describes it, in its ideal form republicanism assumes that cultural identities should have a minimal bearing on citizenship "because they should be transcended through political engagement in a culturally and religiously neutral public sphere and/or subsumed by an inclusive national identity."[155]

While Laborde understands that this is an ideal scenario that fails to take into account real world biases, republicanism can be adapted to bridge the gap between the ideal and the reality of actual states and their institutions that will be historically shaped by religious and other influences. A blend of liberalism and communitarianism, republicanism is perfectionist in that it strives towards a prescribed end in terms of virtues and values embraced by citizens. It is committed to the progressive humanist and secular conception of the person.[156]

Citizens are expected to exhibit civic virtues and attitudes and abide by social norms. She says these are as important as the legal rules and institutions guiding the political community. Freedom and equality are experienced in the political community where persons are protected from arbitrary interference and their equal status is guaranteed. Laborde says attitudes like mutual civic recognition "are fostered, not through forcible inculcation of common values, let alone through the repression of deviance and dissent, but rather through the critical sharing of genuinely public spaces—from political forums to mixed neighbourhoods and common secular schools—where citizens learn to live together, argue and disagree together, and continuously re-invent their imagined collective identity."[157]

Laborde recognizes that "optimal compliance of citizens with republican principles cannot be legitimately required under conditions where those principles are only imperfectly realized and upheld by some provincial institutions."[158] Accordingly, Laborde's approach entails a strategy to emphasize the reformation of the state institutions, so they better reflect the republican ideal. Yet Laborde still expects citizens to be virtuous and not to reject or mitigate the substantive ideals. Laborde says it is "not illegitimate to impose the universal teaching of core civic skills such as personal autonomy in state schools, but only if current curriculum is made sensitive to different ways in which autonomy can be exercised in political societies."[159]

For Canadians, this republican approach is characteristic of liberalism in Quebec. Recently, the province of Quebec passed Bill 21, which prohibits some provincial employees from wearing religious symbols and includes teachers. Why teachers? They are necessary to the province's agenda of inculcating certain values and virtues in all students: values and virtues that foster good citizens. Republicanism prioritizes the political community over other commitments, and civic virtues are expected to trump all others for citizens. It does not claim to be neutral, though it claims that the virtues it promotes are universal. It presumes that all will come to understand that republican virtues are the best for all.

Republican models will vary to the degree they seek to use soft or more direct pressure in promoting adherence to the prescribed values they deem to be necessary to achieve social harmony. Laborde promotes a soft approach through a limited promotion of autonomy in education. However, she does not support private schools. All children, in her view, ought to be taught in public schools to ensure students are taught the values and disposition necessary to sustain the social cohesion necessary for advancing the purposes of the republican polity.

I have used the term *liberal sectarianism* to identify this prioritization of a distinctive set of values that are drawn from one or a few of the comprehensive doctrines that find adherence in a given society. This does not necessarily require the prioritization of the political community over other communities to which citizens may belong (religious or cultural), though it does pressure citizens to publicly adhere to a set of values that conflicts with their core beliefs or to separate their private beliefs from their public comportment.

The liberalism emerging in Canada is more republican as it requires adherence to a more robust public creed reflected in a thicker set of values which all citizens are expected to affirm. This creed is an expression of a pursuit of both individual emancipation (autonomy) and civic integration (fraternity). As we have seen, one of the promises of a liberal democracy is that the government does not take sides in the plurality of beliefs and practices of its citizens and treats all with respect and fairness.[160] It will not punish those who dissent and does not seek to impose its own ideology on others. The embrace of a more robust political creed will compromise this aspiration.

Another promise of a liberal polity is that there be no religious tests for accessing, participating in, or benefiting from government programs. And yet the imposition of an additional set of values is what the government did by requiring applicants for summer grants to sign an attestation, for example. It imposes a form of compelled speech by refusing access to a government program based on whether or not the recipient organization affirms certain values. The expectation that all politicians march in gay pride parades is another indication that there is a certain cluster of values to which those who seek public office must adhere. Similar expectations are not placed on politicians to participate in other cultural or religious celebrations.

Similar to such policies is the promotion of a new understanding of sexual identity and gender that it is fluid rather than being rooted in the male-female duality. An example is the preamble to legislation to ban conversion therapy, which uses the language of cisgender and the language of myth to describe the beliefs "that heterosexuality, cisgender gender identity, and gender expression that conforms to the sex assigned to a person at birth are to be preferred over other sexual orientations, gender identities and gender expressions". When religious beliefs must conform to that which guides and shapes society, some other commitments are exerting authority and legitimacy in society.

Using the two models of liberalism represented by Maclure and Taylor on the one hand and by Laborde on the other, Canadians could opt for a liberal pluralist regime or a republican regime. If the republican route is followed and the political creed becomes increasingly robust and extended beyond the political community, a new hegemony will emerge and those who still adhere to the principles and norms of the old hegemony will become dissenters and nonconformists to the emergent civil religion and its new orthodoxy.

Those of religious traditions or comprehensive doctrines that dissent from the consensus and the majority interpretation will feel the tension of serving two masters. Their religious convictions are tolerated if they are of only private import. All citizens are expected to give allegiance to the consensus in our public lives and engagement. Some of the arguments made in support of the law societies decision to refuse to accredit Trinity Western University's law school, the attestation of the Canada Summer Jobs application, and the College of Physicians and Surgeons decision to require doctors to violate their conscience, are all examples of the dissenters and nonconformists being punished for their rejection of the emerging liberal sectarianism.

As the British Columbia Court of Appeal said in one of the TWU case decisions,

> A society that does not admit of and accommodate differences cannot be a free and democratic society ... This case demonstrates that a well-intentioned majority acting in the name of tolerance and liberalism, can, if unchecked, impose its views on the minority in a manner that is itself intolerant and illiberal. [161]

In the TWU cases, the lower court decisions and the arguments of many parties and interveners display differing views being advanced about the meaning of the state religious neutrality: nonsectarian (benefit is granted despite what is believed), abstinence (benefit is withheld due to religious belief), and qualified neutrality (the religious are benefited if they subscribe to state values).

A common or shared vision is necessary to evoke allegiance to a set of societal norms that enables a society to function well. Either the common principles are the result of a convergence of the respective doctrines of the various significant spiritual forces adhered to within society, or there are two routes; either a consensus needs to be forged and sustained that can operate independent of the spiritual forces, or one of the spiritual forces is embraced and promoted by the state. In both cases the state becomes sectarian.

THE POLITICAL CREED

As any polity, including a liberal one, will be guided by a set of principles and supporting procedures, all states will have a political creed. The issue is how thick or thin the creed will be and whether it is limited to the political sphere and the operation of the state or extends in influence beyond the political community and the state, impacting civil society and the public realm. When the creed extends beyond the political community (citizens and the state), it guides the basis of the common life of the society, and those who espouse other beliefs become the dissenters and nonconformists, while the government embraces the role of defender of the new civil religion.

Perhaps it is easier to the ears to use the word *ideology* rather than *civil religion*. Religion and ideology are different, as religion is oriented to that which transcends, whereas ideology usually has an immanent frame. Both, however, have a faith dimension as Skillen points out above; they espouse norms and a vision of humanity and of history that orient and animate commitments, beliefs, and practices. The spiritual forces identified by Manent can all be described as faiths; they are religion-like, including the ideology of human rights.

An ideology is typically understood as a set of principles or doctrines that explain how a society should be ordered. Recall the public functions Egerton said Christianity played in Canada historically—the priestly, pastoral and prophetic. What religion or ideology now provides these functions? What gives legitimacy to governments and affirms their authority? Who provides pastoral care and prophetically proclaims what is good and evil, justice and righteousness? Who becomes the conscience of the state? Is this now the role of the courts, or politicians and bureaucrats?

The World Lutheran Federation defines civil religion thus:

> Civil religion consists of a pattern of symbols, ideas, and practices that legitimate the authority of civil institutions in a society. It provides a fundamental value orientation that binds a people together in common action within the public realm … Civil religion may also contain a theory that may emerge as an ideology. Individual members of a society may have varying degrees of awareness of their civil religion. It may have an extensive or limited acceptance by the population as long as it serves its central function of legitimating the civil institutions.

It is not necessary that the ideology be broadly embraced by citizens. The issue is the degree to which it influences and shapes key institutions in society.

University of Toronto's Ronald Beiner defines civil religion more narrowly as the appropriation of religion by politics for its own purposes, or the empowerment of religion not for its own sake but for the sake of enhanced citizenship. He contrasts this with a theocracy where religion and state are fused, and liberalism which seeks to give no favor to any religion.[162]

Using Beiner's definition, I don't think there was a civil religion in Canada, as the predominance of Christianity meant the state did not need to appropriate it formally. With a Catholic dominated Quebec and the Protestant dominated rest of Canada, it was best to stay away from any possible direct links between the government and any one Christian expression and, instead, promote a nonsectarian approach to statecraft. Canadian politicians did not wear their religion on their sleeve to ensure the semblance of nonsectarianism, though all prime ministers had ties to Christianity.

If civil religion is the appropriation of religion for political purposes and is usually drawn from the predominant religion adhered to by most citizens, what happens when the majority of Canadians no longer live lives shaped and directed by the Christian faith, and there is no dominant faith that is shared? In the absence of such, there will be a temptation to generate a surrogate. If a deeper cohesion is sought by governments than that afforded by a liberal pluralist approach, if there is a particular vision of the good life or of human flourishing that governments seek to promote, the result will be an increasingly sectarian state. Standards and values will be promulgated which provide the moral framework (a thick political creed) for civil society and a hermeneutic for the sacred texts—those documents that become symbolic of the spirit animating the culture.

One of the many things religions do is to foster or engender a sense of belonging and cohesion; the civic integration identified by Maclure and Taylor requires a sense of fraternity which is expressed in a defined culture and in a commitment to common rules of expression, obedience, and even sacrifice. However, fraternity is difficult to promote within a religiously diverse society. It is incompatible with deep pluralism. Attempts to promote fraternity in a society of deep diversity either misunderstand or purposely ignore deep differences and presume their ideology is universal in its appeal.

CHARTER VALUES

Bob Goudzwaard describes how an ideology emerges when a specific end or goal is given extraordinary significance.[163] The means necessary to accomplish this end become unfettered and norms or values are refocused to become instruments in the pursuit of the end and no longer serve as brakes on the pursuit of the end. Society is mobilized and laws are adjusted to ensure means are available to pursue the end, and any person or community that becomes an obstacle to the end becomes the enemy; the ideology creates scapegoats.

What values do we share as Canadians? What is normative for our society? In Canada, the Charter has gained prominence and is seen by many as a symbol of Canada and its aspirations. As George Grant opined, the Court has become the conscience of the nation. Though the purpose of the Charter is to define the limits of the power of government, frequently it is being held up as a defining feature of Canadian society in a way the British North America Act of 1867 was not. The Charter is treated as an exemplar of Canadian identity, not merely a constitutional brake on the reach of governments. In public rhetoric, and some would argue in its application, what was meant to be a shield protecting us from government overreach is becoming a sword imposing values and acquiescence. What was intended as a constraining document has become an aspirational declaration that gives shape to our common identity. Is the Charter a symbol of the entrenchment of the ideology of human rights that Manent identified as a spiritual force?

Apart from the Charter and the Bill of Rights, Canada has no documents that set out our social contract or the principles that guide our common life together. Prior to these articulations, we had common law precedence and parliamentary procedures established in Britain, and the distinctive common law forged in Quebec. It is then not surprising that the Charter has such prominence. If we apply the idea of a social contract to Canadian society, the Charter would be the most complete articulation of the contract. The Meech Lake and Charlottetown Accords were attempts to further clarify the nature of the contract.

The Charter must be interpreted and applied. Charter values are being increasingly referenced by lawyers and judges as a means to ascertain the meaning of the rights and freedoms laid out in the Charter and other phrases and ideas cited in the Charter but for which the Charter offers no definition or explanation. For example, Section 7 speaks of life, liberty, and security of the person but does not say what this means. The meaning is developed by judges in their interpretations of the terms in their court decisions. Section 7 also speaks of principles of fundamental justice, but again no delineation or explanation is offered in the Charter. Section 1 allows freedoms and rights to be abridged if doing so is reasonably justifiable in a free and democratic society. How do courts decide what is justifiable and determine the breadth of the meaning of the phrase "free and democratic"? And, as the standard interpretation of the Charter is that no freedom or right is given primacy or priority in the Charter, by what standards do judges balance competing freedoms and rights?

The Charter does not self-interpret, as evidenced by the number of times panels of judges have not been unanimous in their interpretation and application of the Charter and the times lower court interpretations have been overturned by courts above. The words used in the Charter require interpretation. By what understanding are they to be interpreted, particularly when judges view that Charter interpretation is a living tree which grows and expands over time?

Bruce J. Clemenger

What is the standard by which the growth is determined? What are the norms and principles, or, in common parlance, what are the values that guide their interpretation? What are the beliefs, the affirmations, the doctrines, philosophy, or ideology, or combination thereof, that guide the interpretation and application of the Charter, particularly when it and its values are not only intended to place limits on our governments but are held forth by some as the definer of who we are as Canadians?

Charter values are increasingly asserted by the courts to provide an interpretive and justificatory framework for Charter interpretation. While they have been asserted by the courts, the courts are not wholly responsible, as judges require some framework of principles to interpret the Charter. If we as a political community of citizens have not engaged in the hard work of identifying and articulating the interpretive framework, or if the background culture is sufficiently diverse and plural that there is ambiguity about the principles, then it is left to the courts to provide the interpretive framework as well as its application to hard cases. Someone needs to fill the vacuum. This is particularly important given the authority and legitimacy ascribed to the courts, and particularly to the Supreme Court of Canada.

When the Charter transitions from being a constitutional limitation to a definer and shaper of the Canadian social contract, hence of our political identity and for some our national identity, it becomes an animator that shapes and directs and takes on a spiritual dynamic. At this point judges take on a priestly role. The judiciary is the arm of the state that determines these charter values: the state names them and gives them content.

When the values are promulgated beyond the political, these charter values become our collective values, our shared values. These values become the definers of what it means to be Canadian. They become the hermeneutic to the Charter. They are the frame within which the Charter is understood and defined and will be used to guide and shape future legislation. That which names and interprets the values is the sovereign.

The task of the political community is the identification of principles forged in debate and dialogue about common purpose, animated by the convictions and wisdom of the various traditions to which Canadians belong. In the absence of a robust and engaged political community, it is becoming the work of the state. Do politicians and the courts in their arguments and justifications appeal to the plurality of doctrines and traditions to which people adhere, or do they appeal to values they themselves assert?

Simply put, the moral ethos that was once fostered by the dominant religious expressions and reflected in the politics of the day (politics follows culture) is now becoming the activity of the state. Rather than being nonsectarian, the state is in danger of becoming increasingly sectarian by privileging a secularist understanding of the good, resulting in the marginalization and privatization of others. In terms of Manent's comment about spiritual forces; what is the spirit, what is the force, driving the new orthodoxy?

THE SEARCH FOR COHESION

For the political community to function, a measure of common commitment and sense of responsibility will be needed to animate the community in its task and provide a sense of cohesion necessary to support, and at times to defer to, the functioning of political institutions and social programs. Historically, cohesion of the political community was rooted in an underlying common religion and the resulting common culture, usually among a people of common race and ancestry. In a society of deep pluralism, the challenge is how to stimulate a collaborative spirit or to generate the civil solidarity necessary to support the redistribution of income or support for national programs. More robust government programs require a greater degree of cohesion. This is in part why the republican approach seeks a stronger sense of solidarity amongst its citizens.

In the case of Canada, when the dominant religion's (Christianity) influence wanes, and a variety of religions or value systems gain adherents with no one religion having authority amongst the majority of citizens, then to move beyond a modus vivendi convergence model and a resulting constitutional consensus requires that a political creed be formulated to provide the basis for the political community that a common religion previously provided (among other elements, the priestly, pastoral, and prophetic functions). The more robust the expectations of the political community, the thicker the creed will need to be. Some set of principles as well as a sense of mission and vision are needed to establish and maintain social cohesion and elicit a sense of camaraderie, as well as provide direction for the future. A common or shared vision is necessary to justify demanding and evoking allegiance to a set of societal norms that enables a society to function well.

The strength of the cohesion necessary will increase as the demands placed on citizens become more onerous. The more minimalist the expectations, the less need there will be. And the more directionally diverse a society becomes, the more difficult it will be for the political community to have a robust sense of common identity and purpose.

To what degree is the state as state responsible for fostering the cohesion and overcome divisions? Or does the responsibility lie with civil society—that is, with communities or institutions within civil society—or is it a shared responsibility?

There is a tendency for governments to take on this task of fostering cohesion, expand it beyond the needs of the political community, and promote a sense of fraternity across society. In part it secures a greater hegemony amongst citizens than would usually be found within a deeply plural society. Another reason is that people need a sense of belonging, and while this was once met through membership in a variety of institutions and associations, as these decline, an alternative is sought.

This network is sometimes referred to as civil society and includes family, neighbourhoods, schools, businesses, unions, religious organizations, missions, legions, theatres, studios, and clubs. It is though these that people find a sense of camaraderie and belonging, and some provide a place to gather, provide food and shelter, and other supports. When these come to have less prominence, and as states are increasingly providing parallel supports though government programs, people are becoming more reliant on governments and seek a sense of belonging in their relation to governments, with government agencies being the connector.

Republican liberalism sometimes uses the term *fraternity* to describe the level of hegemony it expects amongst its citizens. However, deep directional pluralism and fraternity conflict. The very notion of fraternity draws its meaning from those bound together by a defined religious calling and practice rooted in a shared belief and common mission. Even within the Roman Catholic faith, there are a myriad of fraternal orders whose differences are pronounced enough to warrant separate fraternities, even though they all adhere to the same Christian tradition.

Fraternity is too high a goal in a religiously plural society. To sustain a measure of fraternity across religious differences presumes either that all religions are essentially the same and that they share an underlying commitment to certain universal values that overrides the differences, or that religious beliefs and their practices are deemed to be personal and private, and fraternity, or cohesion, requires that the public or civic principles and commitments should trump personal religious commitments, at least in the public square. The citizen as citizen's first loyalty is to the state or nation—loyalty to country then God, not God and country.

As discussed earlier, either the sense of cohesion and common principles of the political community is the result of a convergence of the respective doctrines and the expectations of the various significant spiritual forces adhered to within society, or a consensus needs to be forged and sustained that can operate independently of the spiritual forces (or that privileges one force over the others). If the consensus is established and enforced through law, then when the consensus—or, more specifically, the interpretation of the principles of the consensus—conflicts with the principles of a given religious tradition, then the consensus is presumed to trump the tradition: citizens are pressured to affirm the consensus despite their religious convictions. For those belonging to religious traditions that dissent from the consensus or majority interpretation, they are serving two masters.[164] Religious convictions are tolerated if they are only private and of little public consequence. As citizens, all are expected to give allegiance to the consensus in their public lives and engagement.

6. NEXT STEPS: WHICH PATH WILL BE TAKEN?

As we have seen, Canadian politics embraced a nonsectarian approach to managing and accommodating directional pluralism. Sometimes called principled pluralism or open secularism, this treatment of directional difference seeks to be fair and "neutral". Being neutral poses a challenge because any state will be directed by a series of principles or values, usually articulated in the constitution, and these principles and values will be drawn from one or more sources.

The key then is for the state to recognize that these might result in a bias and recognize the need to accommodate directional differences while honouring the commitment to the established principles. This set of principles, values, and aspirations, what I have been calling the political creed, orients and animates the political community. In many democracies, the political creed informs the procedures by which governments are elected and how they formulate and review laws and policies. When Canada was formed, the British North American Act (BNA Act) of 1867 did not articulate such norms. The 1960 Bill of Rights was a contribution to this articulation, but it was not until the constitution was amended to include the Charter that rights and freedoms were embedded in the constitution.

A republican approach has a greater expectation of cohesion amongst citizens and seeks to foster a sense of solidarity and fraternity across differences. This promotes a sense of inclusion and increases the willingness of citizens to contribute to programs that promote the shared values of the public creed. It builds social cohesion and solidarity and a sense of belonging and allegiance to the state. The rise of nationalism we see in some countries nourishes the same sentiments, though usually around a certain ethnicity or culture rather than values.

A new triad of values are currently being promulgated: diversity, inclusion, and equity. In a country that promotes multiculturalism and is religiously plural, we are a diverse society. We all want to feel that we are part of society (and specifically of the political community) and that we will be treated equally. These values can be interpreted to be consistent with the principle of equal respect and living in a democracy where all are included and have an equal say. However, when these principles are extended to other spheres of life, they cannot be sustained.

Deep differences, be they cultural or religions, mitigate against "inclusion", for example. A culture collapses if its defining characteristics are eliminated to afford inclusion. Some institutions or associations are defined by difference. Universities maintain academic standards and do not admit those who do not meet their minimum standards, and churches have doctrinal statements to which members must adhere and those who cannot are free to find another community to which they can belong.

Likewise, a common culture by definition excludes diversity, as does religion, which entails a uniform belief system. How these principles, or others, are understood and how they are applied in a society of deep pluralism is critical, as is the ongoing conversation about the role of the state and the role of other institutions and associations that make up our society. In times when the institutions of civil society are weak, we must resist the impulse to expect the state to fill the void. The political community is a place of belonging and a source of cohesion, but so too are the other institutions of civil society. It is in these spheres, in places of worship, in families, community associations, and clubs, in places of education, in unions and businesses, that we also experience belonging.

Taylor and Maclure advocate for freedom of conscience and mutual respect as the basic principles of a free and democratic society. This does not mean that we cannot go beyond these in our various spheres of life, in our nongovernmental institutions, organizations, and associations. What they were concerned about is when governments use their power to promote additional norms or values or try to supersede other institutions and become the premier place of belonging and cohesion. Seeking to do so will compromise the nonsectarian nature of the state, as government resources may then be used to promote a sectarian agenda.

To foster an open pluralism, the political creed is best understood as the product of a convergence that is reflected in constitutional documents (such as the Charter). These can be amended, and the terms used in the constitution or other documents that express the political creed are subject to interpretation, and their meaning can change over time. Hence a critical element in any democracy is an ongoing and robust conversation about the demands of citizenship and the role of the state so that each generation owns the political creed, and the pursuit of public justice is understood to be the undertaking of a community and not a task delegated to others. Members of civil society, both individuals and in communities, need to be engaged in this conversation, as well as fostering an ongoing dialogue about Charter values and the principles necessary to sustain a free and democratic society with deep differences.

Religious communities and other institutions, organizations, and community associations that comprise civil society are essential to this ongoing conversation. The political community is but one community to which we each belong. Its creed is a limited set of principles that guide its work and foster mutual respect and freedom of conscience.

OUR CHALLENGE

Two approaches, two regimes of secularism, are operative in Canada that raise certain questions: Will our society opt for a liberal pluralist model by which a convergence is maintained through agreement on shared principles, procedures, and norms of civility that govern our common life together? Will the political community embrace people and their communities who adhere to a variety of beliefs and norms, who enjoy expressive freedom, and who contribute to the public good from out of their respective faiths? Or will we embrace a more republican approach and a new hegemony and accompanying orthodoxy, based on a more robust formulation of values and assertions that are expected to supersede other commitments in not only the political community but also in the public sphere?

The Canada Summer Jobs attestation is indicative of a move to a more republican variant of liberalism, as funding for programs is withheld from organizations whose conscience or beliefs conflict with those of the current government. Likewise, the Supreme Court decision in the TWU case where Charter values were invoked and the denial of conscience to doctors objecting to involvement in euthanasia are also instances of an emerging orthodoxy that presses those dissenting from the new orthodoxy out of the public square and public service.

Liberalism in its sectarian variant can manifest itself in hegemonic ways. As we have seen, some like George Grant and Eric Voegelin see this as an inevitable trajectory of liberalism. As Cécile Laborde has noted, even the form of liberalism that aspires to fairness and accommodation will affirm basic fundamental principles, promote "sacred" values, and have aspirations for all its citizens.[165]

The issue is whether these are "thin" and are supported by those who adhere to diverse comprehensive doctrines. Or will they become so thick that liberalism forfeits its claim to fairness and tolerance and begins to inculcate its citizens into a sectarian set of beliefs and practices, a new orthodoxy of sorts, that is incompatible with principles and practices of other comprehensive doctrines?

With the collapse of Christendom and the Christian hegemony in Canada, a time when Christianity was effectively the public religion and provided the background culture for law and public policy, Canada has two paths it can follow: an open pluralism as described by Taylor and others, or a more republican and sectarian liberalism. A new sectarian hegemony will require an empowering civil religion shaped by a new orthodoxy that will foster the necessary sacred values, sustain the fundamental principles, and animate and direct the aspirations of the political community, and will become punitive to those not subscribing to the beliefs now animating its worldview. An open pluralism defers this to the worldviews adhered to by citizens and requires only a minimal public creed that will guide the political community—both citizens and the state.

The task of advocates of open pluralism is to identify the standards and principles of the political community, including the requirements of civility and the procedural framework and processes that will sustain a convergence among adherents of different doctrines. Based on this consensus of the nature, structure, and ethos of the political community, it will need to deliberate on how thick the convergence must be to sustain a just, collaborative, and peaceful society of willing subjects, not coerced citizens.

It is important to affirm alternatives to the creeping sectarianism while exposing the incompatibility of a new orthodoxy with a truly free and democratic society that accommodates deep directional pluralism, and not diversity for its own sake, in order to respect the freedom of persons and communities to pursue and live out their respective visions of what is true and good. Affirming the dignity of all, tolerating what is not incompatible with the sustaining of the political community formed by the directional convergence and the resulting nonsectarian state, the task is to articulate and continue to refine the principles and procedures that will animate the political community and foster collaboration for the public good.

We can build upon the Canadian tradition of a nonsectarian state and pursue a free and democratic society. The freedoms guaranteed by the Charter in section 2 are qualified by section 1, which enables freedoms and rights to be abridged if doing so is compatible with a free and democratic society. The meaning of "free" will determine how robust will be the freedoms we enjoy as Canadians. Our task is to engage in a deliberative and sustained dialogue with other Canadians of good will to explore the nature of what we mean by freedom in a truly democratic society to which we aspire. As I wrote in *Faith Today*, "for a democracy to work well, citizens must contribute to the consensus and at times challenge or defend it."[166]

The liberal pluralist regime is more conducive to freedom of conscience and religious freedom than a liberal secularist regime. The specter of liberalism inevitably becoming sectarian must be recognized. However, in the current matrix of differing notions of state neutrality, secularism, and Canadian values, the liberal pluralist approach is still defensible and viable as a bulwark against the emerging sectarianism and its orthodoxy. There are precedents for a nonsectarian and impartial state that afford a context within which churches and ministry organizations can flourish and bear public witness.

As I wrote in *Faith Today*,

> Our historic and present-day Judeo-Christian traditions teach a strong work ethic, social responsibility, self-restraint, generosity and compassion, particularly for vulnerable people. As Canadian Christians, we cannot take these norms for granted. We must continue to nurture and proclaim our faith in Christ both in word and deed, a faith manifest in loving God and our neighbour—also made in God's image—as we love ourselves. This critical part of our witness undergirds our pursuit of laws and policies that protect and nurture life.[167]

And further, we do our best when we follow these norms:

> Incarnational living by which we model our lives after Jesus is the beginning of our witness ... our caring for others, our pursuit of justice and standing against the excesses of our culture will attract these secular seekers.[168]

Providing a theological defense for a liberal pluralist approach requires a separate essay. In this work I have attempted to show that this approach can provide a political philosophy in which Christian and other religious communities can live out their faith in an integrated way in civil society, freely engage in the public sphere, and be welcome contributors to advancing the public good.

QUESTIONS FOR STUDY

1) What is the main point the author is bringing to our attention?

2) What themes emerged for me?

3) How do the Courts "think"?

4) Why is it important to be present in Parliament, at Parliamentary Committees and in the Courts?

5) Why is public engagement so important to a healthy democracy?

6) In his 1960s classic text, *The Christian Mind, How Should a Christian Think?* Harry Blamires describes five key principles that make up a Christian worldview.[169] Discuss your views and why you consider them informative to your life and decisions.

    a. Acknowledgment of the supernatural, e.g., the existence of a Supreme God

    b. A holistic view of the self and of service

    c. An affirmation of truth

    d. An awareness of evil, brokenness

    e. A high regard for human beings

7) What is my takeaway?

    a. How do I "think" differently now, having read this text?

    b. How can I get involved, given what I have learned—as a parent and grandparent, at work, in places of worship, and in voting?

EPILOGUE:
FAITH AS PUBLIC ENGAGEMENT:
PERSONAL REFLECTIONS
ABOUT THE AUTHOR

Bruce's first appearance in the *Evangelical Review of Theology* journal in 2003 was published the spring of his appointment to the CEO and President's role of The Evangelical Fellowship of Canada. He wrote this prior to the Board's inaugural ceremony, which was held in the autumn of that same year, guided by elder Mavis Étienne and Rev. David Wells. In journeying these decades, we learn that a lot of individual and collective insights have been gained about how we understand the nature, content, and epistemology of faith *as* public engagement.

In considering the contents of this text, one would be remiss not to capture the life, faith, and service of the author in a more detailed and personable way.[170]

Not many know Bruce's journey in terms of his calling. How is it that one youth, with a willing heart and Bible, reading under the old pine trees on Lake Rosseau in Muskoka, was about to embark on journey with a statesman's capacity and in the sentinel's role for his life trajectory?[171] It gives pause for thought as it begs the same questions he asked at that time: What is faith *as* public engagement? What will this calling in life require in terms of principles, virtues, service, and a dash of one's own personality?[172]

Bruce grew up familiar with what it means to serve in the Christian community and with the vision and mission of the EFC. His father, James "Jim" Clemenger, was sowing seeds in a number of ministries and was also part of a business community that came alongside the founding of the EFC.[173] In 1989, Bruce became a volunteer with the EFC's Social Action Committee to help draft key studies and participate in the growing of networks within the Christian landscape. In 1992, he approached Brian Stiller to become a staff researcher and later that year became Director of Public Affairs. In 1996, Bruce established the EFC's Ottawa office, later known as the Centre for Faith and Public Life.

When Bruce was first invited to put his name forward to become CEO and President, he said no. Not many would do this. He was in the depths of the marriage debates consuming Parliament.[174] The timing did not seem right.[175] I remember affirming: "If it's meant to be, it will have to be in a year." Sure enough, time passed and he was again asked. This time he said yes.[176] No matter the role and while the sun is still shining, he keeps his hand to the plow (mission) and his head focused on the horizon (vision). This is one of Bruce's greatest character assets.

It has been over thirty years since Bruce also embarked on the scholar's journey. At York University he earned a BA (honors) in history and economics. While at York, he studied with Rabbi Sol Tannenzapf, a protégée of Abraham J. Heschel.[177] Rabbi Tannenzapf encouraged him walk further into the call of ministry amidst his interest in economics, history, theology, and politics.[178] And with his questions in hand, Bruce sojourned further to earn a Masters of Philosophical Foundations in political theory from the Institute of Christian Studies (Toronto). He kept to his studies, completing his course work towards a PhD in political theory.

For Bruce, what it means to be an evangelical Christian is that faith as public engagement aligns itself with how the scriptures speak about what it means to be a servant of the Kingdom of God: to witness and participate in a manner worthy of the gospel.[179] Bruce's diplomatic and thoughtful approach is a testimony to one who exhibits faithfulness stemming from 2 Timothy 2:15.[180] This is important to *Christian* faith as engagement.

Bruce's own story unfolded to require his presence and participation in the rooms of power where decisions are made. Over these decades his observations and insights are the result of these firsthand meetings and experiences in a variety of forums, international and domestic.[181] Bruce commented on what this was like,

> It's never predictable, and always the stakes are high... [and] Appearing before the courts of Canada, and particularly the Supreme Court, is a privilege and responsibility ... On this level, Evangelicals have a lot to contribute to the dialogue about the nature of religion and the scope of religious freedom, the sanctity of human life, the dignity of the human person and the care for the vulnerable. By participating as interveners we offer the wisdom of the principles we find in the Word of God, and seek to show how these principles will contribute to the public good, to justice and to peace. It is an important part of Christian public witness in Canada today.[182]

His studies and dialogues on the principles and trends discussed in this text direct our attention to the emerging orthodoxy unfolding within Western democracies and affecting all communities. He is confident that to know "the political paradigm of public engagement is to be able to provide individuals and churches with sound strategies for biblical engagement."[183]

For Bruce, it is about identifying the principles in play, cautioning others about the consequences of the paths chosen, and proposing alternative strategies for the challenges being faced.[184] Faith as public engagement is principled, constructive, reasoned, respectful, dignifying, and at times mixed with wit and humor.[185] Yet principles can also be overlooked, marginalized, rejected, and not always positively affirmed and advanced.

Writing his *Faith Today* columns are times of principled encouragement, education, reporting, admonishment, or sometimes they are laments, appeals for better and sounding the alarm bells on themes encountered in these many faceted situations.[186] And he writes from many relational contexts which can be new or those he's journeyed alongside these decades. Writing from the whole person, he is speaking to EFC affiliates and the public, and these columns are written before going back out into the political and legal arenas where principles of state are battled. His columns amplify the aspects of leading a dynamic organization amongst a large variety of networks within and beyond the evangelical community.[187]

These decades in the sentinel's role, he is always looking from both the peaks and the valleys to new horizons.[188] He resolves to think it through himself and to collaborate with others across denominations, faith groups, and cultures.[189] "It's always about relationships," he says.

His intent remains to be prepared and to prepare others to advocate and embody biblically based life-giving principles as authentic engagement; being ambassadors of God's Kingdom first (Philippians 4:8).[190] And I haven't heard him speak ill of anyone either; "Let's consider the principles and direction forward," he'd say. Finding possible common ground is important to Bruce. It's his pastoral gentle nature, winnowing the wheat and the chaff theoretically and practically.

Not one to personally seek the limelight for himself, his focus is always about harnessing media to uplift the vision and services of the EFC as an organization.[191] Foremost, Bruce and the EFC team focus on showcasing the breadth and dynamic of what it means to be an evangelical Christian across cultures, no matter the needs.[192] "It's what the church as institution and as the body of Christ are doing," he would say, "as that is the vision and mission of the organization in the first place."[193] Building the organization and using technological media wisely as a tool to communicate what it means to be salt and light at home or abroad is important to Bruce.[194]

When it comes to secular media, he does lament, however, the general habit of journalists or producers who bypass any constructive and measured Canadian voices. Rather, they turn to Americans or use dynamics in U.S. politics to frame Canadian expressions of faith and public engagement, unaware of or avoiding the ways in which Canadian evangelicals are politically different. He encourages reporters to investigate what the EFC is doing before selecting guests or producing anything. On one occasion, he said the reporter responded to his admonishment by saying: "We have, and you make too much sense; we need some extremists, so we find one eager for the microphone and lights or we go south."

But when the reporting is civil and accurate, Bruce publicly applauds the media.[195] For example, "There were bright spots in the coverage. *The National*, the CBC TV evening news program, profiled the Elections Kit released by The Evangelical Fellowship of Canada (EFC). In this segment explaining how religious groups engage during elections, viewers learned that the EFC is not a single-issue organization, that the EFC covers a breadth of issues and works across party lines."[196] Giving praise where credit is due, especially to secular media, is important to Bruce.

At times, Bruce is one of a few national religious leaders who embodies the courage to stand alone on matters before the Courts and in Parliament. He knows many people are depending on him when he addresses the media. The EFC is a member-based association comprised of 48 denominations, 78 ministry organizations, 33 colleges and universities, and hundreds of individual churches and is supported by thousands of individuals. He also knows the encounters will be tough. Iron sharpening iron is one thing, but true stature is standing alone when principles are being assaulted rather than debated and when distain manifest towards those holding to such principles is par for the course.[197] He is always thankful for supportive staff and colleagues in those times.

During this time Bruce was also present at key academic or church meetings and conferences, exploring fields of enquiry like political theory and pluralism, law, religious freedom, theology, conscience, and Christian thought. Sometimes he participates as a moderator or chair or as a panelist, or simply as a guest, listening and processing ideas and strategies.[198]

When it comes to this text and the Christian approach to political engagement discussed in Part One, it is not a random theory in play politically or biblically. For Bruce, it is statement of intent as a Canadian Christian seeking to maximize how the Word of God, when handled accurately, can and does speak into realms seen and unseen, and how the unity within the body of Christ glorifies God by its witness in both the content and the "how" of the Kingdom of God and its principles.[199] His 2003 original journal essay and subsequent *Faith Today* columns are expressions of his principled stand into this Western paradigm.[200] These are statements, not commentary or opinions, of one seeking to remind readers of important freedoms and securing public space for individuals, for families, and for religious institutions, which includes the freedom to disagree.[201]

Family or couple time at breakfast is always interesting, to say the least. The cereal box is passed as are questions that are significant in life. What happens when the sanctity of human life, the priority of care for vulnerable persons, or the integrity of religious institutions is eclipsed by the politics of individual autonomy?[202] What is the braking system—the checks and balances—of a healthy democracy?[203] What messages are we, the adults, sending to our children and youth about their dignity and worth?[204] How do we unpack the emergent social and political reality to a child's natural questioning through a biblical worldview when opposition and disagreement are now cause for some serious societal outcasting, in schools, at recess or for careers?[205] What does it mean to be human, and what is human nature? What is rest and play?[206] Who determines identity, belonging, and value in a world that creates scales of justice where some don't hold the balance?[207] What's stewardship versus manufacturing when it comes to the planet?[208] These questions in all their forms touched the heart of Bruce as a father.

It's noticeable that vulnerable human beings are indicators of the pulse of the nation. They are often voiceless and the most affected in political paradigms going or gone awry. Defending principles matters.

The Second World War demonstrated how slippery the slope is when the worth of human beings, the economics of population management, and the ideas and practices of individual autonomy are stroked or collide.[209] Clustering, they migrate to manufacture a new "human" being in worldview and ethics.[210] All ideologies twist scripture and deeply held beliefs, especially the sanctity of human life and caring for the vulnerable, so the upholding and handling the Word of God within a political arena is imperative for individuals and communities.[211] It is especially so for those called into these situations.[212] The question of how to accommodate religious expression within the Western paradigm of political society of religious and cultural difference continues to press for creative understanding and response.[213]

In 2018 and 2019, Bruce envisioned a new role for him and the organization that would include writing the story of the EFC's history of public engagement in the courts and Parliament (Isaiah 30:8). Around the same time, Bruce began to draft what is Part Two of this book, weaving into the story only a few of the sixty court interventions he has overseen.[214] "Let's start with these cases," he said; "this is possible with all I do right now." Burrowing his way past the barn stalls and curious horses and into our sunny tack room, he put up a desk for this project and began to write.

Envisioning this new role, with its duties and responsibilities, Bruce began these conversations with the EFC board (at that time) about what a biblically inspired executive leadership transition for the organization and the Christian community would look like. The organization being healthy, staff morale great and on mission, it was a good time to anticipate future needs and for Bruce to envision his new role that would draw on his expertise. (On January 31, 2023, he will become EFC's Senior Ambassador and President Emeritus).

Bruce is known as one who seeks the best in others, and indeed he likes to empower others to reach their best lives. And he's the same way at home. A loving and involved father to his two daughters, Bruce made sure that he was present in their daily lives and at home on weekends. He made sure he was the one cheering them on, and together we made sure we were at every one of their childhood events. To this day, he is very much present in their daily lives; practically or theoretically in their questions and ideas, hopes and dreams.

Yet it is also a time of change in another new and exciting season for Bruce and our family. His weekend time slots are purposely opening up now to do more speaking, and our girls are moving into their own zones, "freeing Dad up" and, importantly, cheering him on! It's reciprocal; Bruce is empowering myself and the girls, and we him. But also it's about being there for him, celebrating his accomplishments and enjoying his popcorn during football and election nights. In those times he makes it very clear that he will work with any government the people elect; "there's always work to be done." And for those who know him well, sometimes his humour is just downright silly, but his music abilities are still first-rate.[215]

Yet, of faith *as* engagement, public and private, Bruce's biggest personal challenge came to him as a "four-day death watch" when he contracted the Covid virus in 2020. While he was assisting my parents just prior to the Christmas lockdown in 2020, the three of them by happenstance contracted the virus.[216] For several critical days in a Toronto hospital, his life was in the balance. In an initial call concerning how severe and daunting his case was ("He's got about four days to turn this around, Tracy," the chief medical officer said), I was advised to prepare our children for the worst-case scenario. My father was already deceased, my mother in and out of the ER, and with myself and our two daughters, Lauren and Kate, at home in the Ottawa Valley during an unstoppable blizzard, this burden was gratefully shared with our caring community, who rallied around us. For all of us but especially Bruce, it became an opportunity to deepen his faith. This person we know as "Bruce" used this freed-up time to pray for others—staff, the board, friends, family, and strangers.

Messages poured in from around the world from people saying they were praying for him while he was praying for them and their families. He was at peace with God—one that passes all understanding.[217] His ICU doctor, who is the chief medical officer of the hospital, herself a Christian, gave him Psalm 91:4 and prayed bedside with him.[218] Alongside us all, Bruce was trusting God to care for his mother-in-law while walking in the valley of the shadow of death and with instructions from me and the girls to definitely keep walking and to always give thanks to every single person who entered the room.[219]

During this time, the prophetic nature of his calling became elevated and quite visible, even to those outside the community he served. His *Faith Today* articles written during the early part of the pandemic showcased the way in which Christians could face this battle, and his subsequent personal experience aligned to verify those insights spoken months earlier.[220] In his *Faith Today* article entitled: "Walking in the Shadow of Death: Finding comfort as we wait upon the Lord," Bruce "spoke into" what would become our family journey months later.[221] Yet that is the nature of his calling—to be pastoral and prophetic in these decades. Bruce is always being led to see just a little further down the road at what the rest of us may not notice, comprehend, or, at first blush, think significant.

Praise God, Bruce journeyed well. Surrendering the outcome to God at the start isn't easy or anyone's guarantee of more time on this earth, but it does lend to a great faith to face the challenge. And for all of those who rallied alongside him and in our deeply vulnerable time as a family, it became another experience in fellowship and like no other! Among those expressing their own faith *as* engagement, with their best foot forward in this relational sense, it mattered. It gave us all a glimpse of heaven on earth too! And he is absolutely fully recovered from the virus, and that dark wintery time is happily behind us all.[222]

The overall social and political challenges described in this treatise can be each reader's aha moment about Canada, about how we engage as believers in Christ, as followers in His Way, in our communities and country. There are most certainly principalities and powers in play, and it can be the time to understand what it means to speak truth to the powers wisely, and to speak with gentleness or boldness depending on what the occasion requires, always as servants of a King.[223] In so doing, each of us can maximize what the roots of humility and the daily lifeline of mercy and grace have to offer to our children, grandchildren, friends, family, neighbours, colleagues, and decision-makers of church and state. And there is joy!

How do we manifest our faith as public engagement? As a firsthand long-time player, Bruce is inspiring and has a lot to teach us.

As a sojourner, I hope there will be more writing from Bruce as he continues to engage in his new role. In these reflections about the author, readers can know him more personally and his worldview and practices about faith as engagement. It can be as simple as one life who has surrendered all to God, who is sharpening our iron, the way Bruce has sharpened mine too along the way (Proverbs 27:17). He asked me to provide my reflections on his calling as the one who knows him best and who has partnered alongside him these decades with a shared calling from the same Ezekiel text (but a different year and occasion). And he made it convincingly simple: "Our lifetime of studies overlap." My heartfelt message to you, Bruce: We thank God for your life and for your insights into what is happening within Canadian life. We look forward to more writings! Thank you.

—Tracy A.C. Clemenger (BRS, BA [Hons.], MA)

BIOGRAPHY

Bruce J. Clemenger has served on the staff of The Evangelical Fellowship of Canada (EFC) since 1992. In 1996, Bruce established the EFC's Ottawa office which became the Centre for Faith and Public Life. In 2003, he was appointed as the EFC CEO and president. During these thirty years, twenty as CEO and president, Bruce has grown the organization significantly and established two more centres: the Centre for Research on Church and Faith, and the Centre for Ministry Partnership and Innovation.

Bruce is a member of the Interfaith Committee on Canadian Military Chaplaincy and serves on the executive of the Canadian Interfaith Conversation. For sixteen years, he participated as a member of the International Council of the World Evangelical Alliance and served on the Board of the Salvation Army Ethics Centre, and lectured as an adjunct faculty member of Tyndale University College and Seminary, and Trinity Western University. Before joining the EFC, Bruce was the executive director of Samaritans Purse Canada.

In the Courts and on Parliament through these decades, Bruce has appeared before Parliamentary committees more than twenty times and has supervised more than sixty court interventions, thirty of which were before the Supreme Court of Canada. In his statesman capacity and watchman's role, Bruce has worked across the tenure of six Canadian prime ministers engaging in the intersection of faith and public life as a firsthand witness and participant.

As statesman and scholar (PhD cand.), Bruce is an award-winning columnist and speaks and writes on religion, culture, ethics, and politics and has been interviewed by secular and religious media.

Bruce is the father to two daughters, one in her teens and one in her twenties. Together with Tracy, are raising their children on an acreage in the Ottawa Valley. Bruce was born and raised in Toronto, and his childhood family summertime was spent also in Muskoka, with parents very active in church and ministry life. His childhood home was a revolving door of hospitality and stay-overs for missionaries, dignitaries, and politicians. His father, Jim Clemenger, was also one of the early founders of the EFC.

Something playful from Bruce's childhood? Mrs. A.W. Tozer invited three young teens into her home after her husband died. While pointing at different objects, she asked each one what they would like to have. After the other two friends chose, Bruce took his turn and graciously thanked Mrs. Tozer for A.W. Tozer's typewriter—the one on which he wrote *The Knowledge of the Holy*!

ENDNOTES

1. Bruce J. Clemenger, "In the Light of His Kingdom: Going about our Father's business," *Faith Today* (January/February 2022).

2. Isaiah 40:31; Ephesians 6:10-20; 2 Corinthians 5:17-21; Philippians 3:20; Galatians 2:20; Romans 8:28. As believers, we recognize the principalities and powers in play personally and in our service, submitting to Christ, the author and finisher of our faith. Hebrews 1:1-2.

3. Francis Fukuyama, "The End of History," *National Interest* 16 (Summer 1989): 3-18.

PART ONE

4. Francis Fukuyama, *The End of History and the Last Man* (New York: Free Press, 1992), xi.

5. Benjamin Barber, *Jihad vs. McWorld* (New York: Ballantine Books, 1995); Thomas L. Freidman, *The Lexus and the Olive Tree* (New York: Anchor Books, 1999).

6. For example see George Grant, *English-Speaking Justice* (Toronto: Anansi, 1974).

7. Mark Dickerson and Thomas Flanagan's *An Introduction of Government and Politics 4th edition* (Scarborough: Nelson, 1994). Much of this section follows the presentation of liberalism.

8. John Stuart Mill said, "The only purpose for which power can be rightfully exercised over any member of a civilized community, against his will, is to prevent harm to others. His own good, either physical or moral, is not a sufficient warrant."

9. As expressed by T.H. Green: "When we speak of freedom, we should consider carefully what we mean by it. We do not mean merely freedom from restraint or compulsion ... we mean a positive power or capacity of doing or enjoying something worth doing or enjoying and that, too, something that we do or enjoy in common with others." Quoted in Dickerson and Flanagan, *An Introduction of Government and Politics*. See T.H. Green, *Lectures on the Principles of Political Obligation and Other Lectures*, eds. Paul Harris and John Morrow (Cambridge: Cambridge University Press, 1986).

10. In terms of economics, there is a shift from the enforcement of rules of property and trade within a free market to a modification of the market system to ensure the welfare of all. John Maynard Keynes said: "The world is not so governed from above that private and social interests always coincide. It is not so managed here below that in practice they coincide. It is not a correct deduction from the principles of economics that enlightened self-interest always operates in the public interest. Nor is it true that self-interest generally is enlightened: more often individuals acting separately to promote their own ends are too ignorant or too weak to attain these" ("The End of Laissez Faire" [Hogarth Press, 1926], part IV).

11. Lester B. Pearson, "On Liberalism" (1962).

12. John Rawls, *Political Liberalism* (New York: Columbia, 1996).

13. Eric Voegelin, "Liberalism and Its History," *The Review of Politics* 36 (1974/75): 504-520.

14. Voegelin, "Liberalism and Its History," 512.

15. A helpful resource on the themes of liberalism and pluralism is the EFC discussion paper entitled Being Christian in a Pluralistic Society.

16. James Skillen, *Recharging the American Experiment* (Grand Rapids: Baker Books, 1994): 31.

17. H. Richard Niebuhr, *Christ and Culture* (New York: Harper & Row, 1951).

18. Niebuhr, *Christ and Culture*, 136.

19. John Howard Yoder, "Christian Witness to the State," *Institute of Mennonite Studies* 3 (Newton, Kansas: Faith and Life, 1964).

20. Jacques Maritain, *Integral Humanism: Temporal and Spiritual Problems of a New Christendom* (New York: Charles Scribner's Sons, 1996).

21. Gary Scott Smith, ed., *God and Politics: Four Views on the Reformation of Civil Government* (Phillipsburg: Presbyterian and Reformed Publishing, 1989). The main representatives of the four positions are Harold O.J. Brown, William Edgar, Greg Bahnsen, and Gordon Spykman respectively.

22. National Confessionalism is somewhat similar. It argues that all nations should declare allegiance to Jesus Christ in public documents and devise political structures that honour God.

23. Since this essay was first published, this irenic view of Canada has been undermined recently by events such as the Freedom Convoy and other protests that have received global attention.

24. See William Galston, "Expressive Liberty. Moral Pluralism, Political Liberalism: Three Sources of Liberal Theory," *William and Mary Law Review* 40 (1999): 869-907.

25. In my view, as the body, followers of Christ have a variety of gifts and callings and are involved in all areas of life. The church is not a community separate from society, but the body of Christ expressed ecclesiastically. The members of the body worship in churches and participate in all aspects of societal life, seeking to bear witness and call everyone to a commitment to Christ, and to reform all institutions into conformity with Christ.

26. Subsequent to the writing of this essay, Canadian law now allows exceptions to the ban on assisted suicide if certain criteria are met.

27. James Skillen, *The Scattered Voice: Christians at Odds in the Public Square* (Grand Rapids: Zondervan, 1990).

PART TWO

28. Pierre Manent, *Beyond Radical Secularism* (Indiana: St. Augustine's Press, 2016), 103.

29. For another court case on this issue see Bruce. J. Clemenger, "Dealing with Religious Differences: How can we talk about reasonable accommodation for religious symbols in Canadian society?" *Faith Today* (November/December 2015).

30. Bruce J. Clemenger, "Whose Values Shape Our Society?: How respectful and inclusive will Canada be of different belief systems?" *Faith Today* (May/June 2018).

31. For a summary of Manent's view of liberalism see the foreword by J. Seigel in Pierre Manent, *The Intellectual History of Liberalism* (New Jersey: Princeton University Press, 1995).

32. John Rawls set this as his task in his books *A Theory of Justice* (Massachusetts: The Belknap Press of Harvard University Press, 1971) and *Political Liberalism*, two books that have framed the question of how a state can promote a given notion of justice within a religiously and philosophically diverse society for a generation of political and legal scholars.

33. Drawing on the work of Andrew Heywood, Lea David describes an ideology as a belief system, like a secular religion, which offers a worldview that morally defines what the world should be, has a vision of the good society, and promotes political change to advance its notion of the good ("Human Rights as Ideology? Obstacles and Benefits," *Critical Sociology* 6:1 [January 2020]).

34. Press conferences and joint statement by the major religions in Canada are key examples.

35. Bruce J. Clemenger, "The Canadian Way: Canada handles the intersection of faith and politics differently than Britain, France or The United States," *Faith Today* (July/August 2011).

36. Richard Mouw and Sander Griffioen, *Pluralism and Horizons* (Grand Rapids: Wm. B. Eerdmans, 1993).

37. Rawls, *Political Liberalism*, 14.

38. Bruce J. Clemenger, "Tolerance and Respect: Two Key Principles That Can Help Us Live With Our Differences," *Faith Today* (March/April 2017).

39. Bruce J. Clemenger, "Our Election Posture: Challenging indifference and willful blindness," *Faith Today* (September/October 2021).

40. See Susan Mendus, *Toleration and the Limits of Liberalism* (London: MacMillan, 1989).

41. Bruce J. Clemenger, "Conscience in an Age of Choice: Acting with integrity in a morally diverse society," *Faith Today* (September/October 2020).

42. Hannah Arendt, *The Promise of Politics* (New York: Random House, 2005): 93, 96.

43. In 1871, national census revealed 56.45% as Protestants, 42.80% as Roman Catholic, 0.05% as Pagans, 0.03% as Jewish, 0.02% as Mormons, 0.15% as irreligious and 0.49% as unspecified.

44. George W. Egerton, "Public Religion in Canada From Mackenzie King to Trudeau: Entering the age of pluralism, 1945-1982," in *The Cambridge History of Religions in America* 3, ed. Stephen J. Stein (Cambridge: Cambridge University Press, 2012), 28.

45. Egerton, "Public Religion in Canada," 29.

46. John Webster Grant, *The Canadian Experience of Church Union* (London: Lutterworth, 1967), 23.

47. John Webster Grant, *The Church in the Canadian Era* (Burlington: Welch, 1988), 213.

48. Grant, *The Church in the Canadian Era*, 213-214. The "common presupposition" referenced in the quote included a shared understanding of human anthropology and of human flourishing, views that would not be shared in a contemporary directionally diverse society.

49. Grant, *The Church in the Canadian Era*, 216.

50. Blair Fraser, "The Prairie's Political Preachers," *McLeans* (June 25, 1955).

51. Grant, *The Church in the Canadian Era*, 59. Interestingly too, the same decade Christians came together in the founding of the EFC.

52. Speech entitled, "The End of Christian Canada: Past Perspectives, Present Opportunities for Faith and Public Life" by Marguerite Van Die given on September 23, 2002 at Scarboro United Church, Calgary.

53. Grant, *The Church in the Canadian Era*, 240.

54. Egerton, "Public Religion in Canada," 30.

55. Egerton, "Public Religion in Canada," 36-38.

56. For a discussion of the push amongst Canadian political leaders for a religious grounding for human rights see George Egerton, "Entering the Age of Human Rights: Religion, politics and Canadian liberalism, 1945-1950," *The Canadian Historical Review* 85 (September 3 2004), 451-479.

57. Egerton, "Public Religion in Canada," 39-40.

58. Egerton, "Entering the Age of Human Rights," 475.

59. See Egerton, "Entering the Age of Human Rights." The use of the masculine pronouns would not be used in a contemporary report. Unless I am quoting someone else, I use (when appropriate) the non-gender specific language that is inclusive of both male and female.

60. Egerton, "Public Religion in Canada," 26.

61. Egerton, "Public Religion in Canada," 46.

62. Egerton, "Public Religion in Canada," 50 … 60.

63. Pierre Elliot Trudeau, House of Commons debate (December 5 1967), quoted in Egerton, "Public Religion in Canada," 52.

64. Egerton, "Public Religion in Canada," 50.

65. Egerton, "Public Religion in Canada."

66. Statement of the EFC passed by its biannual General Council meeting on February 24, 1981.

67. Egerton, "Public Religion in Canada," 54.

68. Egerton, "Public Religion in Canada," 54. Writing while Stephen Harper (Conservative) was prime minister, Egerton says: "Certainly this seems to be the perception of the Conservative government of Prime Minister Stephen Harper, which eschews any affinity with religious social conservatism," 55.

69. Egerton, "Public Religion in Canada," 54-55.

70. Bruce J. Clemenger, "Muslims and Public Policy: Blaming social change on Muslim immigrants is simplistic and unhelpful," *Faith Today* (March/April 2008): 14.

71. Bruce J. Clemenger, "Church Is Not a Private Club: How should society recognize the uniqueness of religious freedom?" *Faith Today* (September/October 2017). See "Two Dimensions of Religious Freedom: We strengthen society when we help religious agnostics realize they aren't neutral," *Faith Today* (January/February 2017).

72. R. v. Big M Drug Mart Ltd [1985] 1 S.C.R., 350-351.

73. For a description of the changing commitment to the sanctity of human life see Bruce J. Clemenger, "Choosing Between Life and Death: How to promote the sanctity of human life after the Supreme Court decision on assisted suicide," *Faith Today* (March/April 2015); "How Common Beliefs Fuel Assisted Death: When individual autonomy is supported by a gnostic ethic," *Faith Today* (January/February 2019); "A Matter For Equal Protection: Advocating for our neighbours with disabilities," *Faith Today* (January/February 2020).

74. On this development see Bruce J. Clemenger, "Principles To Live By: A public debate on assisted suicide and euthanasia will be one of the next major issues facing Canadian Christians," *Faith Today* (November/December 2005), "From Sanctity of Human Life to Individual Autonomy: Understanding how Canada has changed can help us in the debate on euthanasia," *Faith Today* (January/February 2016): "Loving Our Dying Neighbours: Let's not make a hasty decision about legalizing the hastening of death," *Faith Today* (May/June 2016).

75. Rodriguez v. B.C. (A.G.) [1993] 3 S.C.R., 533.

76. R. v. Big M Drug Mart Ltd. [1985] 1 S.C.R., 336-7.

77. For commentary on some of these issues see Bruce J. Clemenger, "Two Days in June: Are our laws on prostitution and euthanasia outdated?" *Faith Today* (July/August 2013); "But It's My Body!: Canadians of differing religions and philosophies can agree to limits on what we may do with our bodies," (November/December 2013); "Slavery in Canada: Any buying and selling of human life is an affront to the Christian world view – and the principles all Canadians share," *Faith Today* (November/December 2009); and "A Time To Care, A Time To Act: People nearing death need our care and tangible expressions of love," (November/December 2014).

78. John Gray, *Two Faces of Liberalism* (Cambridge: Polity Press, 2000).

79. For an interesting account of confederation as a way to keep the peace by provincializing the political influence of religion (Catholic Quebec and Protestant Ontario) see James Forbes, *Protestant Liberty: Religion and the Making of Canadian Liberalism 1828-1878* (Montreal: McGill-Queen's University Press, 2022).

80. J. W. Grant, *The Church in the Canadian Era* (Vancouver: Regent College Publishing [1972], 1998), 24.

81. Egerton provides a glimpse of the shifts within the United Church in public faith. For a more detailed account see Kevin Flatt, *After Evangelicalism: The sixties and the United Church of Canada* (Kingston: McGill-Queens University Press, 2013).

82. Bruce J. Clemenger, "Three Understandings of State Neutrality: Why not force doctors, school and charities to operate under current social values?" *Faith Today* (March/April 2018): 43, 45.

83. The historical failure of this is heard today among the issues in and the relationship of liberalism (and colonialism) with First Nations.

84. Clemenger, "Three Understandings of State Neutrality," 45.

85. Bruce J. Clemenger, "Unexpected Affirmation: The Supreme Court agrees neutrality is philosophically impossible, which is good news for people of faith," *Faith Today* (March/April 2012), reflecting on S.L. v. Commission Scolaire Des Chenes.

86. S.L. v. Commission Scolaire Des Chenes [2012] 1 S.C.R., 252, 253.

87. S.L. v. Commission Scolaire Des Chenes, 252. See Richard Moon, "Government Support for Religious Practice," in *Law and Religious Pluralism in Canada* (British Columbia: UBC Press, 2008), 217, at 231.

88. Chamberlin v. Surrey School Board District No. 36, [2002] 4 S.C.R. 791.

89. See my commentary on his argument in Clemenger, "Unexpected Affirmation."

90. That we are all believers in something was even popularly echoed in Bob Dylan, "You Gotta Serve Somebody," *Slow Train Coming* (Columbia, 1979). See also Bruce J. Clemenger, "In Word and Deed: Redemption extends to all of life: body, soul, mind and spirit. It involves the renewal of the mind and the healing of the body," *Faith Today* (July/August 2004); and "An Uneasy Conscience: Are we who claim to be Christ-followers truly living out the message of Jesus?" *Faith Today* (September/October 2006).

91. Bruce J. Clemenger, "Advancing Religious Freedom; Several recent court cases are clarifying the scope of our religious freedom," *Faith Today* (May/June 2015): 17.

92. Jocelyn Maclure and Charles Taylor, *Secularism and Freedom of Conscience* (Massachusetts: Harvard University Press, 2011), 10. See Isaiah Berlin, "Two Concepts of Liberty," in *Four Essays on Liberty* (Oxford: Oxford University Press, 1969).

93. Maclure and Taylor, *Secularism and Freedom of Conscience*, 9-10.

94. Maclure and Taylor, *Secularism and Freedom of Conscience*, 13.

95. Maclure and Taylor, *Secularism and Freedom of Conscience*, 13-14.

96. "Being Christian in a Pluralistic Society: A Discussion Paper on Pluralism in Canada," Social Action Commission of The Evangelical Fellowship of Canada (1997), 2.

97. Bruce J. Clemenger, "The Charter: Unchartered Territory?: Let's be articulate and engage fully in public discussions about the Charter and about applying the principles of justice," *Faith Today* (March/April 2007). This was written on the 25th anniversary of the Charter in Canada.

98. Maclure and Taylor, *Secularism and Freedom of Conscience*, 21.

99. Maclure and Taylor, *Secularism and Freedom of Conscience*, 22. See Micheline Milot, *Laïcité dans la Nouveau Monde: Le cas du Québec* (Turnhout, Belgium: Brepols, 2002).

100. Maclure and Taylor, *Secularism and Freedom of Conscience*, 24.

101. Maclure and Taylor, *Secularism and Freedom of Conscience*, 27.

102. Maclure and Taylor, *Secularism and Freedom of Conscience*, 28.

103. Maclure and Taylor, *Secularism and Freedom of Conscience*, 29.

104. Maclure and Taylor, *Secularism and Freedom of Conscience*, 31.

105. Elsewhere, Taylor is more concerned about the positing of an independent ethic and the impact on minorities. See Charles Taylor, "Modes of Secularism," *Secularism and its Critics*, ed. Rajeev Bhargava (Oxford: Oxford University Press, 1998).

106. Maclure and Taylor, *Secularism and Freedom of Conscience*, 34.

107. Ronald Beiner, *Philosophy in a Time of Lost Spirit* (Toronto: University of Toronto Press, 1997), 14.

108. An interesting study would be to explore the implications of these two sets of assumptions in colonization and the formation of Canada. Hobbes and Locke demonstrate there is no one European view, as not all embrace the notion of dominating and subjugating other peoples as opposed to forming mutually beneficial alliances and treaties. See Terry LeBlanc, "A native Canadian question: What aspects of Canadian culture do Western Europeans give up when they embrace Christianity?" *Faith Today* (November/December 1997): 34-35.

109. Taylor, "Modes of Secularism," 12-13.

110. Taylor, "Modes of Secularism," 15.

111. Taylor, "Modes of Secularism," 14. Also see Alasdair Macintyre, *Whose Justice? Which Rationality?* (Indiana: University of Notre Dame Press, 1988). The lectures of French philosopher Michel Foucault, given over many years at the Collège de France, provide a window into how some genealogies of knowledge come to the surface of public consciousness and then dictate social norms—and then how other knowledges come to be silenced over decades or centuries. Foucault quickly became famous for his ideas in the 1970s in America and France. See Michel Foucault, "Society Must Be Defended," in *Lectures at the Collège de France 1975-1976*, trans. David Macey (New York: Picador, 1997); and "Security, Territory and Population," in *Lectures at the Collège de France*, trans. Graham Burchell (New York: Picador, 2007). For a critique of Foucault see Jean Baudrillard, *Forget Foucault* (Massachusetts: M.I.T., 1977).

112. Bruce J. Clemenger, "Discipling the Mind: Christian higher education helps us bear witness to the full implications of our faith in all areas of life," *Faith Today* (January/February 2009): 14.

113. Remarks of the right Hon. Beverley McLachlin, P.C., given at the 2005 Lord Cooke Lecture in Wellington, New Zealand, December 1, 2005, as quoted in George Edgerton in a paper titled "Beautiful Inventions (And some not so beautiful)," presented on June 8, 2006.

114. Conrad Black, *The Canadian Manifesto* (Toronto: Sutherland House Publishing, 2018).

115. George Grant, *Technology and Empire* (Toronto: Anansi, 1969), 114.

116. George Grant, *English Speaking Justice*, 4.

117. Grant, *English-Speaking Justice*, 15-16.

118. Grant, *English-Speaking Justice*, 36.

119. Grant, *English-Speaking Justice*, 36.

120. Grant, *English-Speaking Justice*, 38.

121. Grant, *English-Speaking Justice*, 52.

122. Grant, *English-Speaking Justice*, 61. Grant does not comment on the many parallels of the role Catholicism played, particularly in Quebec.

123. See Paul Kahn's analysis of the demands of a liberal state for sacrifice in *Sacred Violence: Torture, Terror and Sovereignty* (Michigan: University of Michigan, 2008).

124. Grant, *English-Speaking Justice*, 62-63.

125. Grant, *English-Speaking Justice*, 63. See Charles Darwin, *On the Origin of Species*, originally published in 1859.

126. Grant, *English-Speaking Justice*, 63. He says it was the secularized version of Calvinism that was particularly open to the definition of will as autonomy.

127. Grant, *English-Speaking Justice*, 67.

128. Grant, *English-Speaking Justice*.

129. Grant, *English-Speaking Justice*, 68.

130. Grant, *English-Speaking Justice*, 72-73.

131. Grant, *English-Speaking Justice*, 77.

132. Grant, *English-Speaking Justice*, 87.

133. Grant, *English-Speaking Justice*, 83-84. On the impact of the expansion of eligibility of euthanasia on persons with disabilities see Bruce J Clemenger, "A Matter of Equal Protection"; "Conscience in an Age of Choice"; and "A Disability Doesn't Define a Person: We are all image-bearers of God," *Faith Today* (March/April 2013).

134. Grant, *English-Speaking Justice*, 19

135. Grant, *English-Speaking Justice*, 24. Grant did not anticipate a constitutional interpretation of the living tree, and the construction of Canadian values in misinterpretation. Constitutions are not as stable as he suggests, particularly in their interpretation.

136. Grant, *English-Speaking Justice*, 6.

137. Christopher Dawson, *Religion and the Modern State* (New York: Sheed and Ward, 1940), 64-65.

138. Voegelin, "Liberalism and Its History," 504-520.

139. But as we know, science is not "free" and the results, though publicly funded, are often privatized in patentable form and available to only to a few. Often monetary profit guides decisions, not just careers. See the works of the extraordinary scholar David F. Noble, *The Religion of Technology: The Divinity of Man and the Spirit of Invention* (New York: Penguin Publishing, 1999); *A World Without Women: The Christian Clerical Culture of Western Science* (New York: Knopf Doubleday Publishing, 1992); and *America by Design: Science, Technology, and the Rise of Corporate Capitalism* (Oxford: Oxford University Press, 1979).

140. Voegelin, "Liberalism and Its History," 512.

141. Voegelin, "Liberalism and Its History," 507.

142. Voegelin, "Liberalism and Its History," 509-10.

143. Voegelin, "Liberalism and Its History," 515.

144. *Faith Today* raised this question on worldviews, social upheaval, and changes in 1997. See Ryan Bramwell, "Christians in Wonderland: Do we change culture or, like the Cheshire cat, change ourselves and disappear into culture?" *Faith Today* (November/December 1997); and Doug Harink, "In the World But Not Of It," *Faith Today* (November/December 1997).

145. Patrick Deneen, *Why Liberalism Failed* (Connecticut: Yale University Press, 2018), 3-5.

146. James Skillen, *Recharging the American Experiment*, 31.

147. See James Sire's worldview questions for readers to consider. For all sorts of reading levels, this booklet is set at an easy reading level and provides a framework in which to better understand components of a worldview. Also see Ken Badley, *The Challenge of*

Choice (Grand Rapids: Nelson Thomas Learning, 1996); and Brian J. Walsh and Richard Middleton, *The Transforming Vision: Shaping a Christian World View* (Grand Rapids: Intervarsity Press, 1984).

148. John Gray, "The Problem of Hyper-Liberalism," *Times Literary Supplement* (March 30, 2018).

149. Taylor, "Modes of Secularism," 16.

150. Remarks were made at a symposium titled "End of Life, Equality and Disability: A National Forum on Medical Assistance in Dying," held in Ottawa on January 30, 2020. It was sponsored by the Canadian Association of Community Living and the Council of Canadians with Disabilities.

151. For a discussion of atomism see Charles Taylor, "Irreducibly Social Goods" in *Philosophical Arguments* (Cambridge Massachusetts: Harvard University Press, 1995), 127-145.

152. Keyes, "The End of Laissez Faire," part IV.

153. Bruce J. Clemenger, "From Sanctity of Human Life to Individual Autonomy," 16-17.

154. For a fuller critique of this form of liberalism and its assumptions see Michael Sandal, *Liberalism and the Limits of Justice* (Cambridge: Cambridge University Press, 1982).

155. Cécile Laborde, *Critical Republicanism: The Hijab Controversy and Political Philosophy* (Oxford: Oxford University Press, 2008): 2.

156. Laborde, *Critical Republicanism*, 4.

157. Laborde, *Critical Republicanism*, 11.

158. Laborde, *Critical Republicanism*, 13.

159. Laborde, *Critical Republicanism*, 14-15.

160. Bruce J. Clemenger, "Can We Run for Office?: Evangelicals are valuable participants, not pariahs, in a healthy democracy," *Faith Today* (July/August 2005).

161. Trinity Western University v. The Law Society of British Columbia [2016 BCCA], 66.

162. Cited in John Helis, "God and the Constitution: The Significance of the Supremacy of God in the Preamble of the Canadian Charter of Rights and Freedoms," MA Thesis (Ottawa: Carleton University, 2013).

163. Bob Goudzwaard, *Idols of Our Time* (Toronto: Intervarsity Press, 1984), 24-25.

164. Media plays a powerful role in fermenting the majority view. Bruce J. Clemenger, "Misconceptions: Inaccurate portrayals of evangelicals in the news are harmful and unacceptable, but how do we challenge them?" *Faith Today* (September/October 2005); "Have Evangelical Optics Changed?: Election ushers in a new maturity towards evangelicals," *Faith Today* (March/April 2006); and "Responding to Distortions: Rather than being incompatible with Canadian society, evangelicals contribute positively in all areas of life," *Faith Today* (November/December, 2006). Also see David M. Haskell, *Through a Lens Darkly: How the Media Perceive and Portray Evangelicals* (Toronto: Clements Publishing, 2009).

165. Cécile Laborde, *Liberalism's Religion* (Massachusetts: Harvard University Press, 2017), 39.

166. Bruce J. Clemenger, "We Don't Seek to Impose Our Morality: Christians seek the best for our land," *Faith Today* (March/April 2016).

167. Bruce J. Clemenger, "What Principles Sustain Our Laws?: If we don't nurture the principles that sustain our social programs, we may lose the will to maintain them," *Faith Today* (May/June 2011).

168. Clemenger, "In a Secularized Culture," 14.

169. Harry Blamires, *The Christian Mind: How Should a Christian Think?* (New York: Seabury Press, 1963).

EPILOGUE

170. Reflecting on how we go about defining "service" and "activism" *as* evangelical see Bruce J. Clemenger, "Called to Love Our Neighbour: Evangelical activists such as those profiled in the issue are working out their Christian faith and meeting immediate needs. They continue a long and venerable tradition," *Faith Today* (March/April 2010). In poster format see Robert Burkinshaw (selection and text) and Krysia Lear (photo research): "Snapshots: Evangelicals in Canada 1900-2000 – Revivals, Schisms, and Always Something New," *Faith Today* (November/December 1999).

171. Muskoka Woods, formerly Glen Rocks. Looking back, it is a good fit that service like this, and as a calling, begins first in a garden and in solitude by the One who taught us to pray: Luke 5:16; 6:12; Mark 1:35; 6:41, 46; 14:32-42; Matthew 6:5-6; 6:1-34; 14:23; 1 Peter 1:22-25; 5:7. At a young age, Bruce put his faith, life, and destiny into the hands of Jesus Christ (John 14:6). Bruce always asks of himself first what he expects of himself and of others.

172. Her Majesty the Queen HRH Elizabeth II (1926-2022) embodied faith as public service-engagement, as portrayed in the 90th tribute by Mark Greene and Catherine Butcher, *The Servant Queen and the King She Serves* (The Bible Society, HOPE and The London Institute for Contemporary Christianity: London, 2016).

173. Debra Fieguth, "EFC Holds True to its Roots," *Faith Today* (September/October, 2004).

174. Bruce J. Clemenger, "Marriage Refashioned: The participation of all Canadians, including evangelicals, in public policy discussions is needed now more than ever," *Faith Today* (January/February 2005). See also "Why Churches Must Speak: Churches drawn into the public debate on marriage can find guidelines for their witness," *Faith Today* (March/April 2005); and "Reflecting What We're For: As evangelicals, we are called to bear witness to the reality of the lordship of Christ in all that we say and do," *Faith Today* (May/June 2005).

175. To everything there is a season (Ecclesiastes 3:1-11).

176. Interview by Karen Stiller, "Passion and Calling: Faith Today interviews Bruce J. Clemenger, The Evangelical Fellowship of Canada's new President," *Faith Today* (July/August 2003): 14-15.

177. A wonderfully encouraging book that resurfaced for Bruce in 2018 is Abraham Heschel, *The Prophets* (Massachusetts: Hendrickson Publishers, 2007).

178. The writings of A.W. Tozer, and Francis Schaeffer were early reading in his teens and early twenties. Years later, he reflected on Francis Schaeffer in "An Integrated Faith: Remembering the influence of Francis Schaeffer and how he encouraged integral thinking," *Faith Today* (July/August 2006).

179. Bruce J. Clemenger, "Hate Speech Versus Speaking in Love: Christian principles can help as Canadian lawmakers consider the definition of hate speech," *Faith Today* (September/October 2011).

180. John 3:16; Mark 1:15; 2 Chronicles 7:14; Matthew 3:8.

181. When appropriate Bruce wrote about these meetings. See Bruce J. Clemenger, "Meeting President Ahmadinejad of Iran: A meeting in New York City afforded an opportunity to try to understand the controversial leader," *Faith Today* (November/December 2007); "Living In-Between: Palestinian Christians can teach us how the incarnation can influence our daily lives," *Faith Today* (January/February 2008); and "Responding to Jewish Fears: a recent trip to Israel made by Canadian evangelical leaders offers context and perspective," *Faith Today* (May/June 2004).

182. Bruce J. Clemenger, "The Supreme Good: The Charter of Rights and Freedoms has made intervening before the courts an important part of promoting biblical principles in Canadian society," *Faith Today* (May/June 2014), 14.

183. Bruce J. Clemenger, "How Churches Shape Culture: Churches must play both pastoral and prophetic roles," *Faith Today* (May/June 2008); Marianne Jones, "Learning from an Aboriginal perspective on the Gospel," *Faith Today* (May/June 2007): 29, 30.

184. Bruce J. Clemenger, "Accommodating Religious Difference," *Faith Today* (November/December 2018).

185. Bruce J. Clemenger, "Enjoying Life with God: An advertising campaign promoting atheism leads to reflection on enjoyment, self-restraint and how we live out our faith," *Faith Today* (March/April 2009).

186. Bruce J. Clemenger, "A National Reckoning": Kevin Flatt, "Thousands of Missing Lives: The disturbing history of residential schools in Canada," *Faith Today* (September/October 2021): 20.

187. Bruce J. Clemenger, "The Faith That Propels Us Outward: So that we can bless Canada in the name of Jesus," *Faith Today* (June/July 2017); "A Birthday Gift for Canada: What better than a fully engaged evangelical church?" *Faith Today* (July/August 2017).

188. Lisa Hall-Wilson, "Hope and Healing for First Nations and the Canadian Church," *Faith Today* (May/June, 2015): 45-47. Ken Shigematsu, "Why We Do a Land Acknowledgement in My Church: Rejecting heresy, choosing reconciliation," *Faith Today* (July/August 2021): 32-33.

189. Debra Fieguth, "Hearing the Truth, Working for Reconciliation: Evangelical leaders reflect on the TRC report," *Faith Today* (September/October 2015): 48-49.

190. Bruce J. Clemenger, "In the Light of His Kingdom."

191. On the 50-plus years of EFC see Bruce J. Clemenger, "Five Decades of Collaboration: It's time to reflect on how God has blessed us," *Faith Today* (September/October 2014).

192. Bruce J. Clemenger, "What Does Your Church Look Like?: Is it also a community centre and disaster response partner?" *Faith Today* (September/October 2013). See also: Doris Fleck, "Lessons from Calgary's Flood: Is your church ready for an emergency? *Faith Today* (September/October 2013): 18-22. An example is the impact of EFC board members Martin and Eleanor Kreplin during a crisis. Martin, a pastor and trained in critical incident stress management, and Eleanor, an expert in trauma counselling, were literally present when their church was in the immediate lockdown zone in the manhunt for an active shooter in Moncton, N.B. After the lockdown, they opened up the church and offered the opportunity for people in the community to meet and process the event and its impact. "Forgiveness and Healing: The RCMP Funeral in Moncton was a profound experience we can all learn from," *Faith Today* (July/August 2014): 12.

193. For one among hundreds of examples profiling individuals including children and youth, see the article on Carrie Bauer, an elementary schoolgirl of Perth, Ontario, written by Carey Clark, "Bracelets of Hope Ignite a Community," *Faith Today* (May/June 2007): 10-11. On leadership, see Patricia Paddey, "Active Faith: Five Canadians making a difference – examples of believers putting their faith in action. Clinte Curle and Ken McLaren of Ottawa, Jane Halton and Cheryl Bear of Vancouver, and Tim Huff of Toronto," *Faith Today* (March/April 2010): 18-22. For a profile of young adults in business, see Debra Fieguth, "Marketplace Missionaries: Entrepreneurs and Christian thinkers examine how their faith relates to business," *Faith Today* (May/June 2012). The breadth and scope of issues is far-reaching; see Ken Miller, "Lights Camera, Controversy: Following God's call in the entertainment business involves facing a variety of challenges for Canadian Christians," *Faith Today* (January/February 2005): 18-20; and Ben Volman,

"From Newsman to Lieutenant-Governor: David Onley, Ontario's new Lieutenant-Governor, is an evangelical Christian and an activist on disability issues," *Faith Today* (November/December 2007), 18-20.

194. Bruce J. Clemenger, "The Ongoing Impact of Billy Graham: Two of Billy Graham's greatest contributions are his integrity and the international networks he helped to found," *Faith Today* (July/August 2009): "The statements on evangelism and social responsibility flowing out of the Lausanne Covenant (1974) and the Manila Manifesto (1989) are critical in framing a more integrated and socially dynamic faith than what characterized evangelicalism at the turn of the past century ... Now it is no longer personalities but organizations that have this global ability to convene key gatherings ... He used his influence to gather leaders who have set the agenda that defines contemporary evangelicalism."

195. "Should faith-based arguments be banned from the public square? A journalist recently posed this question to me. It's a good one" (Bruce J. Clemenger, "Faith and Public Debate: Should faith-based arguments be banned from public debates?" *Faith Today* [September/October 2012]: 16).

196. Bruce J. Clemenger, "The Canadian Way," 14. It would seem that France "as a vision" is in trouble, experiencing a loss of hope especially for youth while still looking to America to solve these, paradigmatically speaking, driving masses of youth to employment in government (security) as economic systems of industry beyond tourism tied to history or architecture wane. An excellent read on this is Pascal Bruckner, *The Tyranny of Guilt: An Essay on Western Masochism* (New Jersey: Princeton University Press. 2010).

197. Bruce J. Clemenger, "Afraid of Debate: Fear is the only thing preventing a parliamentary debate on abortion law," *Faith Today* (May/June 2013); "Called to Love Our Neighbor"; "To the Edge of Suffering: Has our understanding of Christ's suffering and death become sanitized and routine?" *Faith Today* (March/April 2004).

198. Bruce J. Clemenger, "Someone Is Looking for Your Vote: Now is the time to set the agenda and tone of the election campaign," *Faith Today* (September/October 2015); "Dealing with Religious Differences"; "Hopes for Canada's 40th Parliament: Good governance requires civility," *Faith Today* (November/December 2008). Bruce's tendency is to ask why not discover what candidates believe about faith and politics? This favourite high-impact question is answered personally by each of the four federal leaders including then Prime Minister, the Right Honorable Paul Martin, in "Faith and Politics: Party leaders respond," *Faith Today* (January/February 2006): 18-21. Bruce J. Clemenger. "Fatherhood and the Fatherless: Let's pray and act for Canada's adoption-ready children," *Faith Today* (November/December 2012). Says Clemenger, "Whatever the circumstance, our first response should be one of compassion," 16. Bruce J. Clemenger, "Don't Turn Them Away: Caring for vulnerable children and youth is our shared responsibility," *Faith Today* (January/February 2012).

199. Bruce J. Clemenger, "Generosity, Compassion and Courage: Kingdom principles to live by," *Faith Today* (March/April 2020); "Practicing Generosity: Let generosity become a discipline that characterizes our lives. It will be a form of witness in a materialistic age," *Faith Today* (May/June 2007).

200. Bruce J. Clemenger, "Of Sincere Belief: Canadians enjoy considerable freedom to practice their faith, do Christians take full advantage of it?" *Faith Today* (September/October 2004).

201. Bruce J. Clemenger, "Christian Dissenters in Canadian Society: Advocating for the freedom to engage in the public square," *Faith Today* (September/October 2018); "Integrity in Public Ministry: A challenge against an employer's Christian lifestyle policy

is an opportunity to explain integral Christian faith to a secular world," *Faith Today* (July/August 2008); "Joining Conscience With Respect: Enabling public witness amid diversity," *Faith Today* (November/December 2020); and "Conscience in an Age of Choice."

202. To name a few areas on the sanctity of human life and care of the vulnerable: On children and Jesus Christ see Bruce and Tracy Clemenger, "The World's Greatest Child Advocate," in *Let's Protect Our Children: 18 Faith Leaders Speak Out*, eds. Doug Blackburn and Karen Stiller (Mississauga: World Vision, 2014), 28-31; on parentless children, "A Wake-Up Call: Caring for Canada's children. It is – or should be a national concern," *Faith Today* (November/December 2010). This article marked the launch of the AdoptionSunday initiative at the EFC. Bruce and Tracy Clemenger, "Canada's 30,000 Adoptable Children: How can we help them find home?" *Faith Today* (November/December 2010). On respecting and cherishing human life, see Bruce J. Clemenger, "A National Reckoning"; "Choosing Between Life and Death: How to promote the sanctity of human life after the Supreme Court decision on assisted suicide," *Faith Today* (March/April 2015); "A Matter of Human Dignity: A Supreme Court case requires us to consider our commitment to the sanctity of human life. How dedicated are we to uphold its value?" *Faith Today* (May/June 2009).

203. Bruce J. Clemenger, "Making Moral Judgements: Will we all remain free to make countercultural, faith-based choices?" *Faith Today* (January/February 2015), "Of Church and State: Though churches do contribute to the political life of a nation, they must also understand their role in a democracy," *Faith Today* (November/December 2003). Note: this is Bruce's inaugural year as President, seeking to offer an understanding of the position of the church within a democratic society.

204. Bruce J. Clemenger, "Renewing Canada's Care for Children: The old adage that children should be seen and not heard is not something Christ practised," *Faith Today* (January/February 2011). Also see, the EFC Refugee Settlement Initiative.

205. Bruce J. Clemenger, "Do No Harm: Will medical professionals really be required to kill?" *Faith Today* (July/August 2016); and "Not the Time for Resignation: The legalization of euthanasia and assisted suicide leaves us much more work to do," *Faith Today* (September/October 2016).

206. Bruce J. Clemenger, "Biblical Rest as Leadership."

207. Bruce J. Clemenger, "Too Many Victims: Child neglect and the response of our churches," *Faith Today* (November/December 2016); Chap Clark, *hurt 2.0: Inside the World of Today's Teenagers* (Michigan: Baker Academic, 2011).

208. "The Environment or God's Creation?: The earth must be stewarded, cared for and respected – for it is not ours but God's," *Faith Today* (July/August 2007).

209. Bruce J. Clemenger, "Is Faith Important in Canada?: More acknowledgement is needed in current public discourse," *Faith Today* (November/December 2017).

210. Bruce J. Clemenger, "Commercialization and Its Limits: When confronting the commodification of humans, true progress means affirming the dignity of all and limiting what can be bought and sold," *Faith Today* (March/April 2011); Hannah Arendt, *The Life of the Mind* (New York: Harcourt Brace Jovanovich, 1978); and *Between Past and Future: Eight Exercises in Political Thought* (New York: Viking Press, 1966).

211. Bruce J. Clemenger, "Blessed Are the Peacemakers."

212. Bruce J. Clemenger, "Freedom and Incontestable Anthills: In whom will we place our trust?" *Faith Today* (September/October 2019.

213. Bruce J. Clemenger, "Faith and the 'Values' Debate: Canada – a nation in search of guiding principles," *Faith Today* (January/February 2006); "We're More Than What We Do: Sustaining the principles that shape our laws and impact our lives," *Faith Today*

(January/February 2014); and Matthew Coon Come, "Listening to Idle No More," *Faith Today* (April/May 2013): 29-30.

214. EFC surveys cases across all levels of the courts through their five key areas of focus: the sanctity of human life, care of the vulnerable, family and community, and church and mission and religious freedom.

215. In his twenties and thirties, Bruce loved singing in the Bayview Glen Men's Quartet (Toronto).

216. This family experience with the Covid-19 virus occurred before vaccines were available to hospital staff (between December 2020 and January 2021).

217. Isaiah 26:3; Philippians 4:7.

218. Interestingly, proning is a medical treatment of laying side to side and on the stomach for hours at a time to maximize CO_2 emissions from the lungs. Symbolically, we were reminded that Ezekiel did the same thing!

219. Psalm 23; 1 Thessalonians 5:16-18.

220. Bruce J. Clemenger, "The Scattered Flock"; and "Faith in Unsettling Times: The assurance of the gospel," *Faith Today* (May/June 2022).

221. Five months prior to getting the virus, Bruce wrote: "Walking in the Shadow of Death: Finding comfort as we wait upon the Lord," *Faith Today* (May/June 2020). Also see other *Faith Today* articles by Bruce concerning the pandemic: "God Our Comforter, We Cry Out"; "When Covid Strikes: Resilient praying and caring communities are essential" *Faith Today* (March/April 2021), written after this personal family experience, Bruce acknowledges his father-in-law's death (virally asymptomatic) and it is dedicated to Ken Clark (1930–2020).

222. Bruce J. Clemenger, "Pandemic Leadership: Sound habits for unusual times," *Faith Today* (January/February 2021).

223. See G.B. Caird, *Principalities and Powers. A Study in Pauline Theology*, The Chancellor's Lectures for 1954 at Queen's University Kingston, Ontario (Oxford: Wipf and Stock Publishers, 1956).

www.ingramcontent.com/pod-product-compliance
Lightning Source LLC
Chambersburg PA
CBHW031519270326
41930CB00006B/443